ETHICS AND LAW
FOR THE
DENTAL TEAM

PasTest
Dedicated to your success

ETHICS AND LAW
FOR THE
DENTAL TEAM

Mark G Brennan, BA (Hons) MA AKC DHMSA ILTM FRIPH
Head of the Division of Clinical Education,
Kent Institute of Medicine and Health Sciences
University of Kent in Canterbury

Richard G Oliver, BDS MScD PhD LDS RCS (Eng) FDS RCS (Edin) ILTM
Reader in Orthodontics,
Director of the Dental Education Unit,
and Honorary Consultant in Orthodontics,
School of Dentistry, Wales
College of Medicine, Life and Health Sciences,
Cardiff University and Cardiff Dental Hospital

Dedicated to your success

Egerton Court
Parkgate Estate
Knutsford
Cheshire, WA16 8DX

Telephone: 01565 752000

First edition 2006
Reprinted 2009

ISBN: 1 904627 41 2
ISBN 13: 978 1 904627 41 8

A catalogue record for this book is available from the British Library.

The information contained within this book was obtained by the authors from reliable sources. However, while every effort has been made to ensure its accuracy, no responsibility for loss, damage or injury occasioned to any person acting or refraining from action as a result of information contained herein can be accepted by the publisher or the authors.

PasTest Revision Books and Intensive Courses

PasTest has been established in the field of postgraduate medical education since 1972, providing revision books and intensive study courses for doctors preparing for their professional examinations.

Books and courses are available for the following specialties:

MRCGP, MRCP Parts 1 and 2, MRCPCH Parts 1 and 2, MRCPsych, MRCS, MRCOG Parts 1 and 2, DRCOG, DCH, FRCA, PLAB Parts 1 and 2, Dental Students, Dentists and Dental Nurses.

For further details contact:

PasTest, Freepost, Knutsford, Cheshire WA16 7BR

Tel: 01565 752000   **Fax: 01565 650264**

www.pastest.co.uk   **enquires@pastest.co.uk**

Text prepared by Carnegie Book Production, Lancaster
Printed by CPI Antony Rowe, Chippenham, Wiltshire

CONTENTS

CONTRIBUTORS

Emeritus Professor John Bradfield, MA BM BCh PhD FRCPath

*Bryan Harvey, BDS FGDP

Adrian Longstaffe, PhD BVetMed MRCVS

*Gill Jones, BDS MCDH DDPH RCS (Eng) MPHM

Sheila Oliver, BDS MSc

Jane Williams, BSc PhD
*Key contributors

FOREWORD

Anybody who has spent time on the Professional Conduct Committee of the General Dental Council[1] , as I have done, will know the importance of teaching the areas of Ethics, Law and Professionalism to all of those planning to enter the dental professions. Recently, the GDC completed its 5-yearly round of inspection visits (2003-5) to undergraduate dental programmes across the UK. The main aim of these visits is to determine whether each dental curriculum is 'sufficient' to allow the graduates of that dental school to be eligible for inclusion on the national Dental Register, and thus be able to practise Dentistry within the United Kingdom.

The GDC visitors were guided in their review of the curricula by a framework document for undergraduate dental education – 'The First Five Years'.[2] This document not only provides the benchmark for UK courses but is also widely employed as a work of reference for many other dental training programmes across Europe and indeed worldwide.

At the back of 'The First Five Years' are listed the skills expected of a dentist – the 'Dental Domains'. Prominent amongst these are 'Appropriate Attitudes, Ethical Understanding and Legal Responsibilities' which are given a complete section of their own. Perhaps, this serves to emphasize the importance that national registration authorities such as the GDC, and indeed the whole profession, gives to dentists having a sound working knowledge of this area before being allowed to graduate. Of course, one must remember that the provision of dental and oral care to the public in the 21st century is delivered not by dentists working alone but by teams, all with their own professional responsibilities. Therefore, all those associated with dental care delivery should have a good knowledge of and skills in Ethics, Law and the related topics.[3]

For all of these reasons, most modern dental curricula have threads of 'professionalism and ethics' teaching running through their various programmes from 'day one'. This important book is welcomed since it provides a much needed modern text to support the teaching of these programmes.

Mark Brennan and Richard Oliver have significant expertise and international reputations with regard to their teaching of professionalism, ethics and law to the dental team. Both are well known for their contributions in these and other areas within the Association of Dental Education in Europe[4] and DentEd. To assist in the task which they have undertaken, they have recruited an impressive array of contributors to this book.

The text is well written and easy to read. It states at the outset that it has the intended aim of making accessible to all members of the dental team something that is all to often seen as a 'dry subject'. I think the authors have achieved this aim through an original and stimulating approach to the topic.

I have already emphasized the importance of a book such as this to those learning and acquiring these vital professional skills at the beginning of their professional careers. However, I am certain that it will equally be of assistance to those members of the professions who qualified some years ago and need to polish their skills as part of their continuing learning and development.

This is an important and helpful book which I am sure will rapidly become a standard text for all dentists and members of the dental team – I commend it to you!

Professor Malcolm Jones
Dean of School of Dentistry
Cardiff University.

ABOUT THE AUTHORS

Mark Brennan is Head of the Division of Clinical Education in the Kent Institute of Medicine and Health Sciences at the University of Kent in Canterbury. He is also Honorary Associate Dental Dean in the Postgraduate Deanery for Kent, Surrey and Sussex, and a visiting senior lecturer at Cardiff University's School of Dentistry. He qualified in medical ethics and law at King's College London (MA, 1991). He was a member of the General Dental Council working group which produced guidelines for the education and training of dental care professionals in the UK, *Developing the Dental Team* (GDC, 2003). Mark is co-author of another PasTest book, *The Practical Guide to Medical Ethics and Law* (second edition published 2005). Mark was a DentEd peer visitor to dental schools in Kaunas, Umea, and Sarajevo, and, as an active member of the Association for Dental Education in Europe since 1998, was awarded the ADEE Certificate of Recognition of Excellence in Dental Education in Athens in 2005.

Richard Oliver is Reader in Orthodontics, Director of the Dental Education Unit, and Honorary Consultant in Orthodontics at the School of Dentistry, Wales College of Medicine, Life and Health Sciences, Cardiff University and Cardiff Dental Hospital. He qualified in dentistry at The London Hospital Dental School and worked in practice in the UK and Canada before specialising in orthodontics at the School of Dentistry, Cardiff University. He was responsible for leading Cardiff's dental curriculum change between 1997 and 2005. He has also been involved in European dental education as a DentEd visitor and as an active member of the Association for Dental Education in Europe. Richard was awarded the ADEE Certificate of Recognition of Excellence in Dental Education in Athens in 2005.

DENTAL CONTRIBUTORS

Bryan Harvey is Deputy Head of the Dental Defence Union (DDU) in the UK. He qualified in dentistry at The London Hospital Dental School, has also worked for many years as a general dental practitioner, and continues to take an active involvement in general practice (including a sessional clinical commitment, and chairing the local dental committee in South Essex). Bryan specialises in dental ethics and law, has taught with the authors in Cardiff and elsewhere, and advises DDU members and other dentists. He has published numerous articles on aspects of dental ethics.

Gill Jones is Head of the Dental Care Professional Training and Education Centre and Associate Dean for Dental Care Professional Education in Cardiff University's School of Dentistry and School of Postgraduate Medical, Dental Education. She qualified in dentistry at King's College London and specialised in dental public health. She has taught dental ethics and law and professionalism with the authors to dental and dental care professional students at the School of Dentistry, Cardiff University, and has been actively involved in leading the integration of dental and dental care professional education.

Sheila Oliver is a Lecturer in Adult Dental Health in the School of Dentistry at Cardiff University, and an Honorary Associate Specialist at Cardiff Dental Hospital. She has taught and assessed the learning of ethics, law and professionalism, together with the authors, to student and qualified dental professionals. She obtained the MSc in Medical Education from Cardiff University in 2004.

EDUCATIONAL CONTRIBUTORS

John Bradfield is an Emeritus Professor at the University of Bristol, and was formerly the Professor of Histopathology at Bristol. As a teaching enthusiast, he was an early exponent of the use and development of innovative teaching technologies and computer-assisted learning.

J Adrian Longstaffe qualified as a veterinary surgeon, was involved in veterinary teaching for 20 years, and since the early 1980s has been involved nationally and internationally in the development and support of e-learning in university education.

Jane Williams is Director of e-Learning at the Centre for Medical Education, University of Bristol. Jane has been working in the field of learning technology for over 13 years, much of which has been in the subject areas of medical, dental and veterinary education. As experienced educators with international expertise in e-learning, Adrian, Jane and John have been working together at Bristol University on the use of images and other media to support teaching, learning and assessment in clinical education.

ACKNOWLEDGEMENTS

We dedicate this book to our families, our friends and colleagues in the UK, Europe and further abroad, and – most importantly – to our students and trainees who have all taught us so much about the ethical challenges in dental practice. We acknowledge the invaluable support of our key contributors: Dr Bryan Harvey and Mrs Gill Jones; dental contributor, Mrs Sheila Oliver; and educational contributors, Professor John Bradfield, Dr Adrian Longstaffe and Dr Jane Williams. We are particularly grateful to Professor Malcolm Jones for his support and for providing the Foreword, and to Liz Kerr, our excellent editor at PasTest, who has helped greatly in bringing this book to publication. We also thank Professors Stephen Richmond, Cornelius Katona and Stephen Lambert-Humble, Mr Peter Durning, Mr Richard Herbert, Mr Bryan Webber, Mr Rob Shaw, Mr Barry Mark, Mr Neale Armstrong and Mrs Wendy McCombes for their advice and support. To all of these, we express our sincere thanks and appreciation.

CHAPTER 1
INTRODUCTION
TO THE BOOK

CHAPTER 1
INTRODUCTION TO THE BOOK

What the book is about, what it contains, and who it has been written for

Welcome to *Ethics and Law for the Dental Team*. This new book is designed for use by all members of the dental team – teachers of dentistry and dental professionals, qualified dentists, undergraduate dental students, and dental care professionals (DCPs), a mix hereafter referred to throughout the book as 'dental professionals', for the sake of economy. This mix includes dental nurses, dental hygienists and therapists, technologists, and practice managers, and will also apply to the new DCP categories of orthodontic therapist and clinical dental technician. To achieve this end, we have attempted to write in a practical and accessible way, avoiding – where possible – the usual textbook style and format. We have also involved members of the full dental team in the preparation of this book.

The book provides guidance on the prevailing ethical and professional guidelines on how to practise dentistry in an ethical way, and practical advice on how to avoid many of the common pitfalls. Frequent reference is made to the latest guidance from the General Dental Council (GDC) for dental professionals practising in the UK. Much of this guidance will be relevant to dental professionals working in other parts of Europe and abroad, but – for obvious reasons – we have not attempted to cover ethical guidance or the law relating to other jurisdictions. It is worth noting that both law and ethical guidelines change on a regular basis. This book is intended as a practical guide which can help dental professionals to understand the ethical principles and professional guidelines which apply to the practice of dentistry. Other books are available which give a more in-depth analysis of dental law; details of some of these are given in the resources and reading list in Chapter 10.

It is a GDC requirement that ethics and law should feature in the training of both dental and DCP students. Many of our students have commented that they find it difficult to prepare for examinations in dental ethics, law and professionalism. They often find these subjects less clear-cut than other aspects of dentistry, lacking simple black and white answers. Conversely, many teachers and trainers of dental professionals tell us that they are unsure about how to teach or tackle these areas of dental practice. We have therefore provided some practical advice for both groups, with chapters on how to study and how to teach these important subjects.

The core of this book, applying principles to practice, comprises a set of cases and a set of scenarios, both of which are drawn from 'real life' situations. These cover a range of topics, and are intended to illustrate many of the common dilemmas which dental professionals encounter in practice on a daily basis. These include *inter alia* consent, confidentiality, negligence, whistle-blowing, and responsibilities to patients, to other members of the dental team and to society.

We acknowledge that an understanding of and, in some cases, participation in or prosecution of a research or audit project will form part of the training programme for both dentists and DCPs. As a reflection of the increasing importance of these areas to all involved in the ethical practice of dentistry, we have included chapters on audit, research, evidence-based practice, and sections on the dissemination of clinical images and materials; we have addressed many of the ethical considerations associated with these activities.

Finally, we have included a chapter listing a variety of resources on dental ethics and law which readers may find helpful. The authors would warmly welcome any comments or feedback from readers, and will ensure that this is acknowledged in subsequent reprints or editions of this book.

Mark Brennan
m.g.brennan@kent.ac.uk

Richard Oliver
oliver@cf.ac.uk

CHAPTER 2
HOW TO STUDY DENTAL ETHICS, LAW AND PROFESSIONALISM

CHAPTER 2
HOW TO STUDY DENTAL ETHICS, LAW AND PROFESSIONALISM

Study tips, how to pass those examinations, active learning

Far from being a dry subject, ethics and law can be one of the most interesting and exciting parts of the various dental professional curricula. In Chapters 3 and 4 we look at some of the ways in which dental ethics, law and professionalism can be taught and assessed. This chapter takes a practical look at how the same subjects can be studied.

We use the mnemonic PROFESSIONAL to describe an active approach to the study of ethics, law and professionalism.

P – PRACTISE dealing with ethical, legal and professional issues by discussing these with fellow dental professionals; ethics should be an everyday concern for *everyone* involved in the practice of dentistry, not just something that happens to others in other places and does not seem to concern either *you* or *me*. The study of ethics is a requirement for all those involved in dental practice.

R – READ the journals and publications of the dental defence organisations, especially the case studies which describe ethical problems that have been encountered by other dental professionals; READ the publications of the General Dental Council (GDC), especially those that relate directly to ethics, law and professionalism.

O – OBSERVE the practice of qualified dental professionals, especially those who teach and work in your school, dental hospital, clinic or practice; reflect on how they deal with ethical issues in practice; consider how well they communicate with patients, relatives, and colleagues in the dental team.

F – FIND a study strategy which suits you; everybody learns in a different way. Attendance at lectures may be required by your institution and we recommend lectures as a very good means of obtaining some core information, but you may also find small-group discussions, private study, use of the Internet, and informal conversations with fellow students and teachers to be just as helpful in learning about ethics, law and professionalism.

E – EXAMINATION. Past papers with questions on ethics, law and professionalism may be available in your dental school or institutional library. These will help you to understand the areas that the examiners consider important. Remember that law, in particular, will change as a result of Acts of Parliament – both in the UK and in Europe – and the interpretation of the law will change through cases heard in court, just as our understanding of dentistry changes with advances in materials, techniques or research.

S – SEE as many cases as you can in a variety of clinical settings; the key ethical and legal principles applied to dentistry will also apply to medicine and the other health professions. To this end, dental students will want to make best use of attachments in specialties such as oral surgery: all dental professionals will find that contact with medical doctors and students, other health professionals, and with district general hospitals and general medical practice, provides a great opportunity to learn about the generic ethical issues that affect all clinicians (eg consent, confidentiality and communication); conversely, medical staff will benefit from learning more about dentistry and dental practice, about which many of them know very little.

S – SHOW when answering exam or viva questions on dental ethics and law that you have actually read – and that you understand – the latest guidance from the GDC. The documents can be found online or printed copies can be obtained (see Chapter 10).

I – INVESTIGATE what causes dental professionals to get into ethical, legal or professional difficulties. The GDC website is a good starting point, as are those for the dental defence organisations.

ETHICS AND LAW FOR THE DENTAL TEAM

O – ORGANISE your own learning opportunities for ethics and law. Whether you have already qualified as a dental professional or you are still a student, working in a general dental practice, specialist practice, dental hospital or community clinic, think about organising a lunchtime or evening meeting where a range of ethical cases (perhaps some from this book) are presented and discussed by all members of the dental team.

N – NURSE for one another; dental students often perform the role of a dental nurse for one another in clinic, but do not always get the chance to nurse for other student dental professionals (eg hygienists or therapists) or vice versa. We suggest that an excellent way of learning about the roles and responsibilities of someone else's profession is to work closely together and discuss the issues that arise in practice.

A – ASSIST those who teach dental ethics and law to be relevant and up to date in their approach, by sharing your own experiences of ethics and professionalism in practice, whether as students or as qualified dental professionals. This will help considerably to focus future teaching and learning on the issues which present from an early stage of training.

L – LEARN from patients: the questions patients ask, the worries or concerns they express, the attitudes they display towards dental health, their knowledge and understanding of dental conditions, their aspirations and expectations when seeking or considering treatment. An awareness of the importance of all of these crucial issues and a patient-centred approach can help you to become a great dentist or dental care professional.

Conclusion

Finally, a word of warning: please do not expect the study of ethics, law and professionalism to be easy. It is often difficult, confusing, challenging and frustrating to confront these issues; on the plus side, it is also exciting, rewarding, stimulating and fun to engage with what lies at the heart of good dental practice. In the next chapter, we look at how ethics, law and professionalism can be taught and suggest some approaches which will help to make this teaching relevant, effective and interesting for both students and teachers.

CHAPTER 3
HOW TO TEACH DENTAL ETHICS, LAW AND PROFESSIONALISM

CHAPTER 3
HOW TO TEACH DENTAL ETHICS, LAW AND PROFESSIONALISM

Designing curricula, defining professionalism, teaching approaches

When dental students qualify in the UK, many choose to use the title 'doctor', as happens in most other countries around the world. This word literally means teacher, and we recognise that all dental professionals teach one another from a very early stage of their education and training. Indeed, dental students frequently say that they learn as much about practical dentistry from the trained nurses in their dental school as from the clinical professors. One of the most important areas of dental teaching is how to be an ethical dental professional and how to practise ethical dentistry. This chapter aims to provide some practical advice on how to teach the ethics of dentistry and the ethical values of the dental professions. The contributors to this book all have practical experience of developing and delivering programmes for the teaching of ethics in dentistry at both undergraduate and postgraduate levels. A range of case studies is provided in Chapter 6, which give an idea of the myriad approaches that can be taken to the effective teaching of ethics.

Designing an ethics programme

In the School of Dentistry at Cardiff University, the evolution of a new dental curriculum – and the more recent integration of dental care professional and dental training – provided an opportunity to develop a programme for the teaching of ethics and professionalism. Ethics is sometimes wrongly described by both students and clinical teachers as a 'touchy-feely' or a 'soft' subject, when it can and should be quite the opposite. Conversely, ethics can be taught in a very dry, academic way which makes it appear to be abstract and without much relevance to the realities of life in clinical practice. To overcome these obstacles, the authors employed the principles listed overleaf, which can be summed up by the mnemonic PATIENT.

P – Keep it PRACTICAL. Apply theory to practice wherever possible by using cases, illustrations and demonstrations.

A – Use a structured, patient- and learner-centred APPROACH.

T – TEAMTEACH with other dental professional teachers; this provides variety for the students and practitioners, and stresses the value of working with others.

I – Make it INTERACTIVE – use quizzes, buzz groups, student-led debates and discussions, small-group and plenary presentations – and INCLUSIVE so that all dental professional students and practitioners can feel involved and valued. INVOLVE patients, wherever possible, so that students benefit from their perspective on dental care.

E – ENGAGE and involve students and practitioners by encouraging them to describe their own experiences or ideas. EMPLOY humanistic values – create a positive teaching environment in which learners feel safe. Give praise when deserved, and avoid humiliation or other negative behaviour.

N – NEW approaches to teaching ethics, law and professionalism can be learnt by reading journals such as the *European Journal of Dental Education*, the education section of the *British Dental Journal, Medical Education, Medical Teacher*, and the *Journal of Medical Ethics*, or by attending meetings organised by the Association for Dental Education in Europe or the Association for the Study of Medical Education. Further details can be found in Chapter 10.

T – TREAT dental professional students as colleagues from the start of their training, and ensure that they treat dental professional teachers and each other with the same level of courtesy and respect. This encourages the students to feel valued and to see themselves as part of the dental team, and helps them to take responsibility and behave in a professional way.

Developing professional skills for qualified dental professionals

Dental job interviews regularly include questions on ethics and professionalism. Our experience suggests that many dental professionals are keen to acquire further training and education in ethics. These dental professionals are frequently working in the frontline of dentistry, where stress and lack of experience, support and training can lead to uncertainty about appropriate professional behaviour and attitudes. As used to be the case with medical ethics, it has sometimes been assumed that dental ethics is learned and understood through a process of osmosis, by observing what has been called – in a medical context – the 'well-disposed physician' in action. We do not believe this is enough and suggest that many otherwise good dental professionals are sometimes uncertain about what constitutes professional behaviour and good dental practice, and would welcome structured guidance.

Teaching and learning professional behaviour

Institutions have a responsibility to ensure that their students are able to achieve the stated learning outcomes. This section of the chapter presents a variety of approaches to the teaching, learning and assessment of professional behaviour.

Until relatively recently it was assumed that although healthcare students needed to acquire knowledge and skills, and the curriculum was structured for this, the development of professional behaviour was acquired by some obscure osmotic process, which (presumably because it is difficult) was assessed in a most rudimentary manner, if at all. It is clear that this situation is changing because society will no longer accept the 'doctor knows best' attitude from healthcare professionals; patients seek a partnership with their healthcare provider and want to be able to make informed decisions regarding their health and treatment. However, there is no consensus of approach to the task of teaching professional behaviour.

Is professional behaviour a value or a skill – nature versus nurture?

Can professional behaviour be taught, or is it inbuilt behaviour representing the character of an individual? There is no doubt that the attributes of professional behaviour can be learned as a list and recited on request, and that professional behaviour may be observed by or in the trainee. It is the manner in which clinicians approach their patients and practice that provides the evidence. So, can individuals with dubious moral values ever display good professional behaviour? If they know and apply the rules, then the answer may be 'yes'. However, 'knowing the rules' can only take you so far in adhering to good professional behaviour, and, as will be seen in Chapters 6 and 7, 'the rules' do not always exist!

Ethical dilemmas in particular present difficult challenges because they are often not a choice between 'right' and 'wrong', but a choice between 'right' and 'right', or deciding on what is 'least wrong'. Even in an ideal situation the clinician is faced with the difficulty of picking the 'most right' answer. Furthermore, there is a gap between knowing what is right or ethical and actually doing what is right. Developing the mental fortitude to come to terms with such dilemmas is part of the learning process. Reflection upon such decisions with experienced teachers or staff can contribute to the maturation of the decision-making process.

It has been suggested that appropriate professional behaviour is both a skill and a value, and that students and young qualified individuals go through a phase of 'proto-professionalism' prior to the acquisition of clinical wisdom, but this will only come through various stages of psychological and moral development and reflective judgement.[1] Figure 3.1 illustrates this process diagrammatically.

Figure 3.1 Reproduced with kind permission of Blackwell Publishing Ltd.

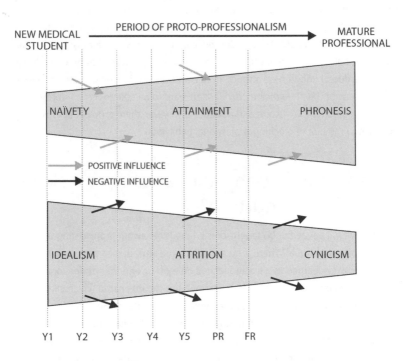

Attainment represents the positive influences on their development, whereas attrition represents the negative influences such as 'unhelpful pedagogical approaches', which can arise from pressures of work in addition to a poorly designed curriculum or lack of support from staff. This suggests that the newly qualified professional will not have all the 'answers' to ethical dilemmas. They will develop a mature approach over a period of time, and they will need a structured approach to their experiences. Opportunities to foster attainment should be encouraged, whereas attritional experiences should be explored in a supportive environment to counteract possible lasting negative effects.

Bertolami[2] argues that the teaching of dental ethics does not change behaviour, or foster the type of reflective activity that might change behaviour. Introspection is a luxury that students are reluctant to undertake, having to focus all their energy on surviving the dental course with its other competing, more concrete demands. He suggests that an ideal time to present and discuss ethical issues is in the period after acceptance to a dental school and before the commencement of the programme. He feels that the future student is full of idealism and has the luxury of time to develop their introspective skills. This approach would provide a suitable introduction to generic ethical behaviour, and, with growing clinical experience and insight, the student could build on sound foundations.

At the School of Dentistry in Cardiff, the authors employed a similar approach. Dental and dental care professional (DCP) students were brought together at a very early stage of training to undertake a fun and practical teamwork exercise involving nothing more complicated than an egg. Over a one hour session, multi-professional student teams were given a supply of basic equipment, and asked to design, build and launch a structure which would protect the egg from damage when it was propelled from one side of the lecture theatre to the other. The ten-minute debrief following the often hilarious competition at the end of the session focused on the question: What has this exercise got to do with dentistry? The students invariably discerned clear links to topics such as good communication (especially listening to colleagues), the effective and economical use of resources, time management, people management, and the need to be gentle and to take care when dealing with something fragile and vulnerable.

Dental students and hygiene/therapy students were encouraged in the first month of dental training to describe what they perceived as the values and virtues of a good dentist or DCP; this proved to be an excellent session each year, which we believe – in nearly every case – helped to confirm their career choice. It also helped to bond the year together, as they recognised a shared experience and common ideas and goals.

However, we concede that such an approach may run into problems with availability of staff, funding, perceived 'curriculum creep', and the potential difficulty of applying messages out of context to students with no insight into the clinical milieu.

Role models – the virtuous faculty

Many would agree that role models during training have had a profound influence on the development of their own professional behaviour,[1,3,4] although the idea that professional behaviour can be 'taught' as well as 'caught' is a challenge to some.[5,6] It has been shown that dentistry attracts a particular personality type that values things that are unambiguous, knowledge-based and useful, and are high achievers, exercising their power for good within the framework of a dental setting.[7] Thus it may be that the role model has, in fact, less influence on professional behaviour than we think, and it is the personality type that values a professional code of conduct (among other things) that attracts people to dentistry and maintains and reinforces their fundamental attitudes and behaviour. It is the refinement and application of the basic traits that come with experience, that is 'taught'. This may be self-taught, taught by example or a mix of both, depending on the learning style of the student.[8]

Chambers[7] also notes that up to 50% of dentists say that they would not choose dentistry as a career again, but only a small number of practitioners actually leave the profession. If these 'dissatisfied dentists' have contact with dental students, might they have a negative impact on the students, or is the inbuilt sense of vocation in the student sufficiently strong to resist the seditious messages? Students who are experiencing self-doubt or staff-generated doubts should be encouraged to discuss their concerns with a respected member of staff.

What should be learned?

The GDC (according to its guidance document to dental schools[9]) expects students to acquire defined knowledge, skills and attitudes. Under the heading of 'Law, Ethics and Professionalism' the student is expected to:

- be able to keep clinical records
- know about their role in obtaining consent
- know their duty of care
- know a patient's rights

- know the permitted duties of dental professionals

- know the regulatory function of the GDC.

Students should be familiar with the legal and ethical obligations of a dentist, their obligation to act in the patient's best interests and the need for lifelong learning and professional development.

More recently, the GDC has produced *Standards Guidance* booklets in a series[10] that replaces its document, *Maintaining Standards*. These booklets are, *Standards for Dental Professionals* (the core guidance document), *Principles of Patient Confidentiality*, *Principles of Patient Consent*, *Principles of Dental Teamworking*, *Principles of Complaints Handling* and *Principles of Raising Concerns*.

Another GDC document, *Developing the Dental Team*,[11] anticipated the recent change in the Dentists Act 1984 to register all members of the dental team, and to regulate their activities by training according to educational criteria (learning outcomes) that define their knowledge, skills and attitudes (competencies). The team, collectively known as DCPs,[12] includes dental nurses, dental hygienists, dental therapists, dental technicians, clinical dental technicians and orthodontic therapists. All members of the team have similar ethical and behavioural learning outcomes.

The above list of dental professionals does not cover all the members of the team. Others who make a substantial contribution to the smooth running and success of a practice include receptionists, practice managers and cleaners. In a hospital setting, the professional expertise of dental radiographers, pharmacists, dental illustrators and photographers, and other colleagues are crucial to the effective provision of dental care and dental education. These individuals will also be expected to behave in a professional manner, and it is the responsibility of the employing dental practice, clinic or hospital to ensure that they understand their obligations, particularly in relation to confidentiality.

How to assist the learning

In the five-year period of a relatively sheltered undergraduate programme, many of the ethical dilemmas that a practitioner will face during his or her practising lifetime will not arise as a direct learning experience for the student. Consequently, a structured approach to the topic is most suitable, supported by active learning in the clinical environment.

In the UK, all the dental defence organisations publish journals or other documents that illustrate the various medico-legal situations faced by their members. These scenarios can provide the basis for discussion with students. Teaching packs covering some of the common problems are also available. There are several advantages to a structured approach:

- Development of learning outcomes provides a clear focus.

- What has been covered is clear.

- When it has been covered is clear.

- Who has responsibility for the delivery of the topic is clear.

- Why it has been covered is clear.

- Careful selection of trigger material can provide generic learning opportunities.

- All students will have had equality of access to the learning opportunity.

- Use of reflective log books will reinforce and embed the theoretical teaching with clinical experience, ie there will be learning in context.

- The student will be able to identify theoretical situations that have not been reinforced by practical experience. This information may be of value to a vocational trainer.

- Assessment can be linked to the learning outcomes.

Communication skills have been identified as one of the key issues in the development of a professional mien. In New Zealand, students undertake a communication skills course that involves workshops based on video recordings (initially of different communication skills techniques, subsequently of students interviewing simulated patients), reflective exercises, and assignments.[13] In Pittsburgh, USA, an approach has been adopted that involves 'service learning' and reflective journal writing. The service learning takes place during the first two years of the course (pre-clinical), and is non-dental in nature. This is reported on in a short reflective journal which is assessed. Rubin believes that this develops students' compassion, righteousness, propriety and wisdom.[14]

Provided that the student has a phased introduction to the clinical environment, a structured introduction to various aspects can be planned. A single block of teaching placed at any time during the course is unlikely to be of great value. At the beginning of the course some of the messages will have little or no resonance with the student.

In the middle or at the end of the course they will be able to relate to some situ
but others will still lack resonance, and they may have already encountered situ
for which they were unprepared. A trickle approach seems more appropriate, with
short bursts or mini-blocks at significant points during the course, followed by
opportunity for self-reflection and discussion with a member of staff, and the
opportunity to put the messages into practice. These opportunities can be divided
into the time:

- prior to access to clinical records

- prior to provision of dental care

- during and after provision of dental care.

Prior to access to clinical records students should understand the importance of
confidentiality, the ways in which confidentiality may be breached, and the
importance of good clinical records and their status as a medico-legal document.
Norwell[15] has proposed 'ten commandments' for satisfactory record keeping:

1 Write legibly.

2 Include date and time.

3 Sign your name (and PRINT it legibly afterwards).

4 Do not use abbreviations.

5 Do not alter an entry or disguise an addition.

6 Do not use offensive, personal or humorous comments.

7 Check everything written in your name.

8 Reports should be seen, evaluated and initialled before filing.

9 Do not discard records.*

10 Understand the law relating to access to records.

*Ideally, records should be kept indefinitely. This is unrealistic and so contemporary
advice is that, generally, records should be maintained until 10 years after the end of a
treatment episode, or until the age of 26 years if it is a child's record. Different
categories of patient require different minimum retention periods.[16]

The establishment of good practice may be assisted by the students using records to
build case reports as part of their course work, or as an audit project to raise standards
of record-keeping across the dental hospital.

Prior to provision of dental care further subdivisions are possible, eg issues surrounding consent may be covered prior to rotation through the general anaesthetic area; and the special circumstances surrounding consent for minors and special-care dentistry patients covered in the relevant clinics, as may the responsibilities of general dental practitioners who refer children for dental treatment under general anaesthesia. Rotation through the general anaesthetic area provides an ideal opportunity for learning about the practicalities of obtaining consent.

During and after provision of dental care provides the active learning opportunities where students may put into practice their prior learning and subsequently reflect on it.

The approach to learning given above suggests that there should be repeated small learning episodes during the clinical programme for legal, ethical and behavioural topics that begin prior to clinical exposure. This is also an ideal time to learn about relatively routine issues surrounding communication with the patient and with the referring General Dental Practitioner. It provides an opportunity to practise referral techniques for opinions and/or treatment in other dental or medical disciplines. This gives the student an opportunity to discuss aspects of a good referral face to face with the person to whom they will refer in future. Furthermore, there should be opportunity for students to reflect on their clinical experiences, with the support of staff who can help the student put these experiences in context.

Zarkowski and Graham[17] have described their structured approach to teaching and learning in ethics and law. The course is spread over four years of the course, commencing in the first year. The course described in the article appears to be an eclectic mix of professional behaviour and clinical governance.

Conclusion

In the next chapter, we will see how ethics, law and professionalism can be assessed.

CHAPTER 4
HOW TO ASSESS DENTAL ETHICS, LAW AND PROFESSIONALISM

CHAPTER 4
HOW TO ASSESS DENTAL ETHICS, LAW AND PROFESSIONALISM

Ideas, techniques, practical examples and approaches

Educational assessment means to judge or measure whether learning outcomes have been achieved by the learner; in the context of dental ethics and law, we assess whether appropriate knowledge, skills or attitudes have been acquired and can be applied to practice. As with other aspects of the dental programme, professional behaviour may also be assessed by both formative and summative means. This chapter will start with the assessment of professionalism or professional behaviour.

In common with assessment of knowledge and skills, there is no single, universally agreed means of assessment of professional behaviour. As noted elsewhere in this book, it is relatively easy to identify unprofessional behaviour, but much less easy to say why it is unprofessional and to reach a decision on whether this behaviour is sufficiently dysfunctional to merit failure in a summative assessment or even disciplinary action. Veloski et al.[1] have reviewed of a range of methods used for assessment. It is clear from their paper that assessment is frequently targeted at limited aspects of professionalism, and the purpose of many of the papers on the assessment of professionalism has been to evaluate programmes rather than students following the programme.

In assessment of professional behaviour, general principles should be followed:

- The assessment should be linked to learning outcomes.
- It should be consistent, reliable, valid, fair and representative of a real situation.
- It should be accompanied by feedback.

It is a challenge to develop assessment strategies that fulfil the above criteria and are also robust. Nevertheless, the competence of a professional individual includes knowledge, skills and *attitudes*, so it is important that professional behaviour is assessed.

Assessment drives learning – does it drive behaviour equally?

It is worth considering that patients are often so grateful for access to NHS dentistry that they will tolerate behaviour by practitioners that, given greater choice of provider, they would find unacceptable. Opportunity for assessment will come from a variety of sources, including written tests of various types, *viva voce* tests, self-assessment, 360-degree appraisal, reflective portfolio, objective structured clinical examinations (OSCEs) and SCOTs. The trickle approach to learning professional behaviour described above is in keeping with the idea that both learning and assessment of professional behaviour should begin as soon as possible. Prior to clinical exposure, knowledge of the requirements of record keeping, may be tested for example.

Factual recall of lists is a level-1 activity and is appropriate during the early stage of a course. There remains the problem of setting a pass mark or standard. Is it 'satisfactory' to know only 50% of, say, Norwell's ten commandments (see p. 21). If so, which 50% are important, or does that not matter? A level-2 question related to Norwell's ten commandments might be: Choose five of Norwell's ten commandments and explain why they are important. A level-3 question might be: Choose three of the six principles of practice in dentistry enumerated by the GDC (see below), and for each provide an example of a clinical situation that illustrates your understanding of what is meant by that principle, and how you would manage that situation.

Professional behaviour in students can be assessed by monitoring attendance, punctuality, time management, preparedness, teamworking, recognition of their own limitations and their response to feedback. Assessment of an individual student's response to a hypothetical ethical dilemma can be made at a *viva voce*, or through an OSCE or SCOT station. Such ethical dilemmas may be based on the six principles of practice in dentistry enumerated by the GDC:[2]

1 Putting patients' interests first and acting to protect them.

2 Respecting patients' dignity and choices.

3 Protecting the confidentiality of patients' information.

4 Co-operating with other members of the dental team and other healthcare colleagues in the interests of patients.

5 Maintaining your professional knowledge and competence.

6 Being trustworthy.

Day-to-day clinical supervision provides an ideal opportunity for contemporaneous assessment and feedback. It can be difficult, however, for clinical staff to spend time actively and accurately observing, when they are often busy in the clinic themselves. Furthermore, staff may be reluctant to confront students who demonstrate 'unprofessional' behaviour, and may be uncomfortable imposing their own values on students.[3] It is well recognised by dental and dental care professional teachers that some students, who might cause concern among their peers, their patients and the trained dental nurses in a clinic, are particularly adept at displaying a professional persona whenever a supervisor is within range.

In addition to clinical supervisors, experienced DCP colleagues are also a useful source of information, particularly in relation to the teamworking aspects of professional behaviour, and the student's approach to, and management of, their patient. Chairside assistance offers an ideal opportunity to make judgements regarding these attributes and can form part of a 360-degree appraisal mechanism. Other contributors to a 360-degree appraisal include laboratory and/or instructor technicians, staff in radiography and audio-visual aids departments, receptionists, patients and peers. Some reports suggest that peers welcome the opportunity to make assessments of their colleagues, but under their own terms and conditions.[4,5] The use of multiple raters for assessment of behaviour seems to be a practice that is gaining ground.[6–8] We suggest that, although potentially valuable, 360-degree appraisal must be used carefully.

Reflective ability is an integral part of being a professional. Dr Jean Ker, Senior Lecturer at Dundee University has described three levels of reflective ability:

Level 1 – Can describe relevant evidence of progress from experience.

Level 2 – Can evaluate relevant experience as evidence of progress.

Level 3 – Can identify and re-evaluate their own learning needs.

Examples of good and poor reflectors at each level are reproduced over the next three pages, with the kind permission of Dr Ker.

Test of reflective ability – a measure of professionalism

Level 1 – Describes relevant evidence of progress from experience

Table 4.1 gives some indicator statements of written evidence you would expect to find in the outcome summaries of an excellent reflector and of a poor reflector at level-1.

Evidence of excellent reflector (level 1)	Evidence of poor reflector (level 1)
Describes relevant experiences in context of outcome Eg *'My orthopaedic attachment gave me the opportunity to develop'*	Absence of detail in summary (too generalised) Eg *'The doctor has certain attributes important for the practice of medicine'*
Summarises experience of progress in relation to outcome Eg *'Over year 4 my history-taking skills progressed ... as shown by ...'*	Evidence given based on authority Eg *'The grades I achieved demonstrate how well I have done'*
Personalises the descriptions of their evidence Eg *'The way I remedied this problem ...'*	Emphasis on quantity – how much they have done Eg *'The 12 clerkings and the number of clinics I have attended show how well I have progressed'*
Links experiences Eg *'During my psychiatry and general practice attachments ...'*	No evidence of linking between specific examples Eg *'Provides a list of activities done'*

Table 4.1.

Level 2 – Evaluates relevant experience as evidence of progress

In reading through the student's reflective summary sheets, identify whether the student is able to analyse and evaluate relevant experiences which provide evidence of their progress towards the outcome. Table 4.2 gives some indicator statements of written evidence you would expect to find in the outcome summaries of an excellent reflector and of a poor reflector at level 2.

Evidence of excellent reflector (level 2)	Evidence of poor reflector (level 2)
Discriminates between usefulness of experiences Eg 'In particular, the theme-based SSM provided the opportunity to ... which is useful because ...'	No comparison between experiences made in determining progress Eg 'I found careful organisation to be the secret to this outcome'
Interprets progress through examples Eg 'My communication skills improved during Phase 3, speaking to people from different ethnic and cultural groups ... enabling me to feel more confident'	States progress with indiscriminate/diffuse evidence Eg 'I feel I have achieved this reasonably well since I passed my fourth-year exams'
Explains progress using supportive evidence Eg 'My own style and approach to clerking developed from both my own practice during my elective and observations of others in clinics'	Analysis of outcome rather than own progress Eg 'Self-care and control with time management are important aspects of this outcome'
Analyses specific factors from experience contributing to progress Eg 'The ward round helped me to identify from the discussion why the decision to withhold treatment from a patient was made in relation to ... which enabled me to understand the ethics framework we had learnt'	Opinion of own progress stated with no supportive examples Eg 'I accept criticism constructively ... I think people find me easy to get along with'
Explains own opinion with supportive evidence Eg 'I think that I have progressed in decision making and reasoning because the following examples ...'	

Table 4.2.

Level 3 – Identifies and re-evaluates own learning needs

In reading through the student's reflective summary sheets, identify whether the student is able to identify, on the basis of their experience, their own learning needs. Assess whether they are able to re-evaluate their progress in learning in relation to the outcomes, taking into account their experiences in different clinical settings. Table 4.3 gives some indicator statements of what written evidence you would expect to find in the outcome summaries of an excellent reflector and of a poor reflector at level 3.

Evidence of excellent reflector (level 3)	Evidence of poor reflector (level 3)
Awareness of own gaps and difficulties in learning/awareness of development of own strengths Eg '*I have become more organised in relation to my presentation skills, which has helped to ...*'; '*I have tried to keep up to date by ... although ...*'	Weaknesses not identified. Strengths not clearly identified in relation to outcome Eg '*I have never encountered any difficulty in this area*'
Recognises with hindsight multiple solutions Eg '*It would have been better if the treatment of this patient had been discussed with a senior colleague and I learnt that there could have several ways to address ...*'	Lack of insight into current level of competence in relation to career stage Eg '*I am competent to be a doctor*'
Identifies problems/inconsistencies in experience of outcome Eg '*I performed better in my surgery PRHO shadowing than medicine because ... which affected my progress in this outcome ...*'	Lack of awareness of continuing development Eg '*I successfully completed all the tasks in my surgery PRHO apprenticeship*'
Re-evaluates own approaches by discussing alternative strategies Eg '*Another way I could have learnt about how to deal with this ... would have been to either ... or ...*'	No awareness of dynamic nature of own competence Eg '*I am competent to be a doctor*'
Recognises dynamic role of external factors on own life-long learning Eg '*I have tried to develop a balanced approach to life to keep both my physical and mental health*'	
Formulates a plan for development Eg ' *I realise graduation is just the beginning and I have attended a seminar on making career choices based on evidence*'	

Table 4.3.

Assessing dental ethics, law and professionalism

One of the objections detractors will sometimes make regarding the teaching of ethics is that it is all about opinions, completely subjective and therefore impossible to assess. Of course, this objection is clearly nonsensical as there is a considerable body of knowledge, as well as ethical guidelines, statutory regulations and laws which a dental professional must know. Furthermore, well-informed knowledge of the prevailing legal opinions helps to make the law work in practice. In the next section we provide some ideas on how ethics and law can be assessed in a range of settings. In later chapters we provide a wide range of ethics cases and teamworking scenarios which can be used by dental professional teachers and students for assessment and self-assessment.

Ethics and law are open to a variety of assessment approaches: written, oral and practical.

Trigger questions

Here we present some of the sample questions we have used with first-year dental, hygiene and therapy students, either as a *viva voce* (oral) examination or as a written examination. In all of the model answers below, students who showed that they understand the importance of recognising the limitations of their knowledge and understanding would be rewarded, especially if they say that they would seek help and guidance from others within the profession. For all answers we would reward the students' written or oral communication skills, ie they should be lucid, audible, clear and concise in their answers.

Question 1

A mother presents with a 7-year-old child with active caries in deciduous and permanent molar teeth. In addition to obtaining a diet history, you also recommend fluoride supplementation. The mother responds that she has read recently that fluoride causes cancer and she will not use it.

How would you deal with this situation?

Answer

We would expect students to refer to the GDC guidance document, *Standards for Dental Professionals*, which states that a dentist or dental care professional should:

- put the patient's interests first and act to protect them

- respect the patient's dignity and choice.

The student should refer to the dentist and DCP's roles as teachers, and possibly discuss who has the right to consent for treatment, recognise the three-way relationship: mother, child, dentist. They should indicate that they would explain, in a non-confrontational manner, the safety issues surrounding fluoride, and the benefits to be gained from fluoride supplementation, being sure to include the child in the conversation. This covers the expanded notes in the guidance document – listen to patients and give them the information they need, in a way they can use, so that they can make decisions. This will include:

- communicating effectively with patients

- explaining options (including risks and benefits)

- giving full information on proposed treatment and possible costs.

Question 2

An adult attends your practice with toothache. A restoration (filling) is the treatment of choice, but the patient demands extraction of the tooth.

How would you deal with this situation?

Answer

The answer to this question should refer to the GDC principles as detailed above, as well as the guidance contained in the *Principles of Patient Consent* document which says:

- For consent to be valid, the patient must have received enough information to make the decision. This is what we mean by 'informed consent'.

- Find out what your patients want to know, as well as telling them what you think they need to know.

- Do not pressurise the patient to accept your advice.

- Patients have a right to refuse to give consent for an investigation or treatment. If they do so, you should respect this decision.

In addition, examiners should expect the student to show a flexible approach to the situation, and not display the arrogance of 'I know best'. The student should want to explore the reasons why the patient wants an extraction. The student should be aware of their own professional autonomy, the need to act in the best interests of the patient and to do no harm. They should understand that they should make arrangements for a second opinion (without rancour) if agreement cannot be reached.

Question 3

A patient of another practice comes to you as an emergency, complaining of pain. On examination you notice several examples of what you consider to be poor quality dentistry, some of which require relatively urgent attention.

How would you discuss this with the patient?

Answer

Seek clarification from patient about their previous dental history (How long since they last attended? Have they missed appointments since then? Did the previous dentist say there was more work to do? Have there been any recent changes in lifestyle/diet?). In his or her answer, the student should refer to the following GDC principles, stating the requirements of a dentist or DCP:

- If you believe that patients might be at risk because of your health, behaviour or professional performance, or that of a colleague, or because of any aspect of the clinical environment, you should take action. You can get advice from appropriate colleagues, a professional organisation or your defence organisation.

- Treat all team members and other colleagues fairly and in line with the law. Do not discriminate against them.

- Maintain appropriate standards of personal behaviour in all walks of life, so that patients have confidence in you and the public has confidence in the dental profession.

In other words, the student should make it clear that they would not bring the profession into disrepute without full knowledge of the facts.

Conclusion

These initial scenarios offer an educational 'springboard' for the assessment of ethics, law and professionalism in subsequent phases of the dental and DCP curricula. The cases and scenarios provided in Chapters 6 and 7 are more complex and require a greater level of prior knowledge.

CHAPTER 5
PRINCIPLES OF DENTAL ETHICS AND LAW

CHAPTER 5
PRINCIPLES OF DENTAL ETHICS AND LAW

Key principles, the role of the General Dental Council and its requirements of dental professionals, consent and confidentiality, and the taking and use of sensitive clinical images

Why bother with ethics at all?

The cynic might say that all of this emphasis on teaching and learning ethics, law and professionalism is a complete waste of time. Ethics is, surely, just a matter of common sense and conscience, isn't it? The fact that someone has been selected for training as a dental professional in the first place means that they must have the right background, attitude and approach, to be trusted to behave in an ethical way. And, as they will undoubtedly be surrounded by highly ethical and professional teachers and trainers during their training in the dental hospital, clinic or practice, how could they not pick up good ethics as they proceed to qualification? Well, the cynic would be wrong, and perhaps dangerously so. The one thing that is sure about common sense is that it is not common at all; conscience is even less reliable as the main guide to ethical practice.

Few people in dentistry share exactly the same combination of upbringing, outlook, values, beliefs, moral or religious, and cultural, social and educational backgrounds – all of those attributes which might contribute to an understanding of what is ethical or unethical. Nor will all dental professionals share an identical experience of clinical education; this, patently, will vary from person to person, and from setting to setting. We have discussed in earlier chapters how a structured and integrated approach to the teaching, learning and assessment of ethics, law and professionalism can ensure that ALL dental professionals are provided with the tools they need to appreciate, understand and apply principles to practice. This chapter aims to provide you with some of these tools.

As a starting point, you might find it helpful to consider what are known as the 'four principles of bioethics'. These were first formulated by two American philosophers, Tom Beauchamp and James Childress, and are sometimes known as the 'Georgetown Mantra' as both were academics in the Kennedy Institute of Ethics at Georgetown University (Washington DC, USA), when they wrote the first edition of their book, *Principles of Biomedical Ethics*. Briefly, the four principles are as follows:

- **Autonomy** – self-determination, the right to decide what should happen or not happen to us; the right to information about a condition, its diagnosis and prognosis, and to say 'yes' or 'no' to a proposed course of treatment (informed consent); the right NOT to have things done to us without that consent.

- **Beneficence** – doing good, acting in the best interests of patients or others.

- **Non-maleficence** – the central message of Hippocrates was above all to do no harm (*primum non nocere*). In a dental context, this would include a dental professional not undertaking a procedure or treatment for which he or she has not been trained and is not competent to perform.

- **Justice** – treating people equally and fairly, being accountable for one's actions or inaction. This principle applied to dental practice would include the need to ensure that all patients had access to at least a basic level of dental care, regardless of income and social status. The just provision of dental care would require that dental professionals should never discriminate unfairly against those who present themselves for treatment and oral healthcare.

We are not suggesting that the four principles are the only ethical approach dental professionals will wish to use, but we do believe that they provide a helpful structure for discussing and responding to ethical dilemmas in practice. They provide a starting point for ethical debate and are widely recognised by other health professionals around the world. There has been considerable debate (which is ongoing) in the academic world, evident in a range of bioethics journals and conferences, about whether the four principles are sufficient to deal with the complexity of healthcare ethics, but we believe dental professionals might find them helpful while recognising that they are not the be-all and end-all of philosophical theory in ethics. These four principles will be revisited and applied in Chapter 9, and referred to in Chapters 6 and 7.

At the risk of being accused of appearing to 'dumb down' the principles which follow, we suggest that there are some 'rules' for ethical behaviour which most of us learnt at an early age; these are not culturally specific and are necessary for a civilised society to exist and survive. We might call them 'the kindergarten rules' but what is applicable to small children remains equally applicable to adults, and to dental professionals:

- **Don't tell fibs** – Tell the truth, be trustworthy.

- **Don't hurt each other** – Take care that your actions or inactions do not harm others, do not be reckless and know your own limitations.

- **Don't tell someone else's secrets** – If patients entrust their secrets to dental professionals, it is because they believe that those secrets will be protected and treated with care.

- **Don't take things without permission** – If, as a dental professional, you intend to extract part of a patient, eg a tooth, make sure you have the patient's consent.

- **Be kind to each other** – Treat others with at least the same care and consideration with which you would expect them to treat you (the so-called 'Golden Rule' in the Judeao-Christian tradition) or, wherever possible, treat others as they would wish to be treated (what has been called the 'Platinum Rule').

These kindergarten rules, out of context, could appear very simplistic but in fact, and on further investigation, they underpin much of the advice which follows and which can be found in the General Dental Council (GDC) standards and other ethical guidance.

Ethics, law and professionals

A professional person is subject to both the law and a professional code of ethical conduct, unlike a trade or business person who – in most cases – is subject only to the law. In a memorable episode of the American television series *Frasier*, the radio psychiatrist Frasier Crane defines ethics as being 'what you do when nobody else is watching'. This definition is especially true for dental professionals as in many instances the patient is totally unaware of the standard of treatment that has been provided. In a survey carried out for the British Dental Association, 85% of patients said that they trusted their dentist. In some circumstances the nurse or other dental care professional working with, or seeing treatment carried out by, a dental practitioner will be the only one who knows whether, for instance, any decay was left at the bottom of the cavity. A dental professional seeing a colleague's patient may find evidence of poor treatment or unmet treatment needs. We will look at this issue in more detail later.

The General Dental Council

The role of the GDC in the UK is to register qualified dental professionals, set standards of dental practice and conduct and assure the quality of dental education. The GDC also ensures that professionals keep up to date, responds to and deals with patient complaints about a dental professional, and works to strengthen patient protection. The GDC states that:

> 'as a dental professional, you are responsible for making sure that you are familiar with and understand the current standard which affects your work and any relevant guidelines issued by organisations other than the GDC.'

You should also be aware of the available sources of evidence to support that current standard, and that you should apply your up-to-date knowledge and skills in an ethical way. The ethical guidance to which dental professionals need to adhere is set out by the GDC in *Standards for Dental Professionals* and the accompanying booklets. In the preface to *Standards for Dental Professionals*, the GDC states that its aim is to 'protect patients, promote confidence in dental professionals and be at the forefront of health care regulation'.

It is vitally important that before any dental professional carries out any treatment they have ensured that the patient fully understands the procedures that she or he is about to undergo and that – if a dental professional is delegating treatment or making a referral – the person to whom that referral has been made should be suitably trained

and qualified and capable of carrying out the planned treatment. If a d
professional delegates another person to obtain the patient's consent,
still be responsible for making sure that – before any treatment is star
has been given sufficient time and information to make an informed
given appropriate consent. Consent is a continual and dynamic process and, during
the whole time that a dental professional is treating his or her patients, there should
be ongoing discussions to ensure that the patient is fully aware of the position in
relation to their treatment.

Currently, the accepted age of consent is 16 years for those who have the necessary
capacity at that age, and 18 years for those who don't (merely attaining the
chronological age is of itself not sufficient, because if a person lacks capacity at age 18
or over they may be incapable of giving valid consent). Lord Denning, in *Hewer* v
Bryant (Court of Appeal 1969), said:

> 'The common law can, and should, keep pace with the times. I should declare, in
> conformity with the recent report on the Age of Majority, that the legal right of
> a parent to the custody of a child ends at the eighteenth birthday; and even up
> till then, it is a dwindling right which the courts will hesitate to enforce against
> the wishes of a child, the older he is. It starts with a right to control and ends
> with little more than advice.'

Gillick competence and consent – how law is made in practice

In 1985 the House of Lords gave judgment in what has become known as the
Gillick case. This concerned a mother of ten children from Wisbech in
Cambridgeshire, Mrs Victoria Gillick, who sought an injunction against her Health
Authority to ensure that none of her children would be given contraceptive or
abortion advice or treatment without her prior knowledge and consent until they
were aged 16. The Law Lords held that a child under 16 could give valid consent to
medical treatment without parental knowledge or agreement ... provided the
child had capacity (intelligence, maturity and understanding) to give consent. For
'Gillick consent' to be valid, the child must have capacity, the proposed treatment
must be in the child's best interests and every reasonable effort must be made to
persuade the child to involve a parent/legal guardian.

Gillick v *West Norfolk and Wisbech AHA* (1986) AC 112, [1985] 3 All ER 402, (1985) 2
BMLR 11 (HL)

especting patients' dignity and choices

The GDC points out that:

> 'Good communication is extremely important to enable patients to participate fully in their choice of treatment. Patients should be able to understand the risks and benefits of the different treatment proposals. Patients should be treated fairly and there should be no discrimination against patients or groups of patients because of their sex, age, race, ethnic origin, nationality, special needs or disability, sexuality, health, lifestyle, beliefs or any other irrelevant considerations.'

It is essential for dental professionals to listen to their patients and to ensure that they are given information in a way that they can understand. We all have two ears, two eyes and one mouth; sometimes in clinical practice the proportions get mixed up, and as dental professionals there are times when we operate more in 'transmit' mode than 'receive'. Effective explanation requires at least as much listening as talking. Different patients may require different ways of having options explained to them. It is vitally important that patients are given the full information in relation to their proposed treatment and the costs.

Lord Justice Lawton said:

> 'Most practitioners do use reasonable care, so they have nothing to fear from the Law; but all practitioners have to obtain the consent of their patients to treatment. I now appreciate that for most practitioners the important legal problem is not negligence but the obtaining of consent to treatment.'

The GDC sets out in the guidance booklet, *Principles of Patient Consent* further details of the main ethical principles for the practice of dentistry:

- **Informed consent** – That is, the patient has sufficient information to enable them to make a decision.

- **Voluntary decision making** – The patient should not be coerced into making any decision.

- The patient should have the **competence** to make an informed decision.

Protecting the confidentiality of patient information

Confidentiality is a cornerstone of all good relationships and good dental practice. Dental professionals are privileged when patients divulge information to them, and they should ensure that this information is kept confidential and used only for the purpose for which it is given. It is vitally important that patients understand which aspects of the information they give to a practitioner may be disclosed and the circumstances under which they may be disclosed. The GDC booklet, *Principles of Confidentiality*, details the requirements for a dental professional to maintain patient confidentiality.

Being trustworthy

A number of surveys have shown that dental professionals are well trusted by the public in the UK, and all dental professionals have a duty to ensure that they are able to justify that trust by always acting honestly and fairly. Dental professionals should maintain an appropriate standard of personal behaviour and be aware that if their behaviour is inappropriate this may have an effect on their registration.

Everyday dilemmas

Ethical and legal dilemmas are often not the headline-grabbing events that people expect them to be; rather, a dilemma is frequently something that occurs in everyday practice, which is perhaps ignored as it does not appear to present significant risks. We suggest that it is exactly these situations which dental professionals should examine and reflect on, as they provide an opportunity for the principles of ethics and law to be applied.

In dentistry, the use of images is such an example, bringing the ethical principles of consent and confidentiality into sharp relief. Dentistry is, of course, a highly visual craft. Until recently many dental professionals would obtain and freely make use of images in diagnosis, treatment, audit, research and teaching. Frequently, minimal effort was made to disguise the identity of the patient concerned. But guess what? The many publications – including tabloid newspapers and glossy magazines – that run quizzes and competitions to identify celebrities under the heading of 'spot the smile' may have already decided the issue for us: it is clear that merely placing a black bar over the eyes of someone's face does not stop that person from being identified. In the next section, our colleagues, John Bradfield, Adrian Longstaffe and Jane Williams provide some timely and helpful guidelines and practical tips for the ethical and legal use of images in dental practice.

A checklist approach to the ethics of taking and using sensitive clinical images

Ethics is about behaving considerately and professionally. Legality is about obeying the law. Acting legally is essential but not enough. We all need to behave considerately and professionally beyond the minimal legal requirements. One of the consequences of this is that we ought, as far as possible, to try to think through issues before an event rather than in the heat of the moment. Ethical checklists help in this process by providing reminders of the things that we might need to consider. As with the rest of the book, in this section we do not set out to provide prescribed answers. Such is not the nature of ethics. We do, however, provide some guidance and practice tips which might help dental professionals to consider the issues involved in the taking and use of sensitive clinical images.

This section derives from the findings of a study from the University of Bristol, where the use of ethical checklists is proving to be a helpful way for practitioners to work out the most appropriate answers for their own specific needs. Behind the seemingly straightforward act of taking a photograph of a patient, there are all sorts of issues that would not immediately come to mind at the time. Here is the first:

If I take a picture of a patient, do I need to ask consent?

Answer – if it is a sensitive clinical picture you do.

Which immediately begs the second question:

What is a sensitive clinical image?

This is our first check.

What are sensitive clinical images?

Currently, most medical and dental practitioners use the General Medical Council (GMC) guidelines, as does the GDC. In short, sensitive clinical images are those in which the patient is identifiable. In dentistry, this is particularly relevant for orthodontists who often need pictures of the patient's full face. The GMC guidelines also remind us that there are other ways of recognising people, such as tattoos or jewellery, which brings us into the grey area of pictures of a whole set of teeth. From a forensic point of view, this can form the basis for legal identification. From a day-to-day, practical point of view, at present it is unclear whether such an image should be regarded as identifiable to the individual.

Just as ethical opinion in general is constantly evolving, so it is with the taking and use of pictures of patients. The current position is that the taking and use of pictures of patients requires formal patient consent only if the resulting pictures are identifiable. However, many people are coming to regard the issue as one of privacy and respect, rather than strict anonymity.

Practice tip

It is best to ask for consent whenever a picture is taken, regardless of whether or not the resulting image is recognisable.

- Get into good habits and always explain what is involved.

- If in doubt, ask consent, and record the consent.

Now for an important principle.

How do the ethics of obtaining patient consent for taking a picture differ from those for obtaining consent to perform a procedure?

The general principles of best ethical practice are the same. These are well covered elsewhere in this book. But there is one crucial difference in emphasis. Although you are asking for consent to do something at the time – to take the picture – the main permission that you are seeking is to use that picture in the future. And it is those possible uses in the future that need to be thought through beforehand – that is where the important issues lie.

Which brings us to our next sets of checks. First, two checks which relate to taking pictures.

Where are the pictures being taken?

Most dental clinical pictures are taken either in an individual practice or in a hospital setting. The general principles are the same. The practice may have its own rules. Otherwise it is up to you to formulate your own good conduct. In a dental hospital there may well be formal policies and guidelines, as well as hospital consent forms. If there are, you are obliged to follow these guidelines.

What about mobile phone cameras?

For once the answer is easy. It is not permitted to take pictures on mobile phones, not only because the phone with its pictures could be lost or stolen but also, more importantly, because it is all too easy to transmit the picture to someone else by mistake.

Now we come to the checklist for what you do with the pictures.

Where will you store the picture?

The patient, quite rightly, assumes that we will ensure the same level of confidentiality and privacy as for patient records. That means taking the digital images from a practice camera and storing them securely within the practice. There would rightly be some unease at the thought that we might take them home on a personal camera or laptop; and perhaps even more unease about having them on a laptop that could be left in the car or on a memory stick that could be dropped.

Back in the practice, pictures need to be indexed and stored with any linked information (metadata). At any time subsequently, any patient can change their mind and ask for their pictures to be removed. The practice needs to have an index system that can allow this.

Images for audit

For orthodontic work in particular, audit requirements may necessitate giving auditors access to images, and copies may be sent digitally. The same general principles of confidentiality apply as if these were patient records. Afterwards, the auditors need to destroy their digital copies.

Presentations at conferences

The arrival of the digital age has changed everything. We take images to conferences, not as glass slides in our pocket, but as images on laptops and in memory sticks. Sometimes the images are emailed to the conference organiser prior to the actual meeting. If the images are identifiable to the patient, then it is important to ask oneself whether the patient consented for this particular use.

Books or scientific articles

Most publishers have well-formulated policies and guidelines regarding recognisable images. Our responsibility as custodians of the images is to be aware of these and to read the small print. If the onus is on us, we need to make sure that we have appropriate consent and, if necessary we have to go back and re-ask for appropriate permission.

Teaching

Dental teaching uses lots of images, and some of these may be identifiable. For face-to-face teaching, this is not highly contentious. But nowadays images are digitised and often delivered via a digital network (e-learning), for the learner to access from many different locations, including halls of residence or even via the Internet. Images can easily be downloaded, even when there are rules against this. Although the issues remain the same as previously, the risk of offence is much increased. For all new pictures, proper informed consent for taking pictures that might be used for teaching involves the practitioner explaining what this might mean in the digital age.

If the images are uploaded to an e-learning network, this is likely to be hosted by a university or dental hospital that may have its own policies and guidelines. It is worth checking who is legally liable if something goes wrong. It may be you.

And what about all those favourite images that you have been using for years? For most it is likely that no adequate consent was obtained and the identity of the patient has long since been forgotten. Clear guidelines are available through the GMC website. In essence they add up to this: If the person is recognisable, there needs to have been consent.

Practice tip

It is no longer acceptable just to blank out the eyes with a black bar and hope for the best.

Now for something entirely different.

Who owns the pictures?

Pictures (or any record, electronic or otherwise, that has been obtained by the practitioner, including radiographs or study models) taken in a dental practice belong either to the practice or to the individual practitioner. Note that this is dissimilar to medicine where the record is not the practitioner's property but that of the state, and will follow the patient. It should be easy enough to check in your practice, but don't be shocked if the head of your practice has never even considered the question. Pictures of patients taken in an NHS hospital in the UK during the course of patient care usually belong to the hospital trust. This means that permission is needed to take copies away for publication or teaching.

When you move from job to job or practice to practice, the issue of legal ownership is ambiguous. Strictly speaking, you should probably seek permission to take your teaching images with you. In practice this is not usually done. Don't bank on this *laissez faire* attitude lasting for ever.

So long as the context is one of not-for-profit education and training, the legal risks are low. But remember, this is not a blank cheque for bad behaviour.

Practice tip

Ask yourself – would the patient (or a national tabloid newspaper) be shocked if they knew what you were proposing to do with the patient's pictures?

Before	After
Think before you start	Think before you use
Remember reading this chapter	Remember reading this chapter
Think through why you know want the picture now	Store as patient records
	Do I own the copyright?
Think through what you might use the picture for in the future	Do I have properly informed consent for this particular use?
If in doubt – ask for consent	
When you do, make sure that the patient understands what they are consenting to	

Table 5.1 Summary checklist.

Conclusion

This chapter has provided an introduction to ethical and legal principles. In the next two chapters, we will be applying these principles to a range of authentic 'real life' cases and scenarios based in dental practice.

Who can give consent?		
	Yes/No	Comment
Patient> 16 years	Yes	
Patient < 16 years	No – but ...	'Dwindling right' of parents prior to age 16. (Gillick Competence) It is good practice to seek the support of the patient as well
Mother	Yes	
Father	Yes	If married at time of conception, birth, or some time after birth. If unmarried, may acquire right to consent by legal adoption. If there is a difference of opinion between mother & father regarding treatment which cannot be resolved, advice of the court should be sought
Brother / Sister	No	May be consulted in real emergency
Uncle / Aunt	No	May be consulted in real emergency
Grandparents	No	May be consulted in real emergency
Childminder / Au pair	No	
School teacher	No	
Local Authority	Yes – but ...	Local authority may be gIven parental responsibility if the child is in their Care or under an Emergency Protection Order
Patient who lacks capacity < 18 years	No	Those with parental responsibility may give consent. It is good practice to seek the support of the patient as well
Patient who lacks capacity > 18 years	Yes	No one else can consent on their behalf. Necessary treatment should be provided that is in the patient's best interests. Good practice to consult relatives
Temporary incompetence e.g. judgement affected by pain, drugs, alcohol etc. Unconscious patient	Yes – but ...	Try to help patient understand options & make informed choice. Good practice to consult relatives. Provide sufficient treatment to save life. Good practice to consult relatives.

People on this list other than parents may acquire responsibility by being appointed a l~gal guardian. Where there is doubt, legal advice should be sought.

CHAPTER 6
DENTAL ETHICS AND LAW IN PRACTICE

CHAPTER 6
DENTAL ETHICS AND LAW IN PRACTICE

Applying ethical and legal principles to dental practice

In the preceding chapter you will have read about some of the ethical and legal principles which underpin dental ethics and law, and in this chapter we will look at how many of the ethical and legal responsibilities of the dental professional are applied in practice.

Case 1 – Following guidelines and applying principles

A patient with a cardiac problem, which requires antibiotic cover, is due to have treatment shortly. The dentist is rather concerned as he has heard that there are some new GDC guidelines which appear to be different from those in the Dental Formulary; *however, he has not read them thoroughly – indeed, he thinks he might have thrown the GDC booklet away by mistake. He expects the practice manager has got a copy somewhere.*

Which guidelines should the dentist follow?

To successfully defend a claim of negligence a practitioner will need to show that she or he followed current teaching and practice and referred to guidelines that were current at the time. Before prescribing antibiotic cover you should consult with the patient's general medical practitioner and/or cardiologist to determine what the appropriate regimen is. Ignorance of the law – or of the relevant guidelines – is not a defence; a dental professional is expected not just to be aware of the latest GDC guidance, but to ensure that the principles are understood and applied to their everyday practice. The GDC clearly states in *Standards for Dental Professionals:* 'If you cannot give a satisfactory account of your behaviour or practice in line with the principles explained in this booklet, your registration will be at risk.' In this same booklet, the GDC sets out the principles for the ethical practice of dentistry. A dental professional is expected to apply the following principles:

- Put patients' interests first and act to protect them.

- Respect patients' dignity and choices.

- Protect the confidentiality of patients' information.

- Co-operate with other members of the dental team and other healthcare colleagues in the interest of patients.

- Maintain your professional knowledge and competence.

- Be trustworthy.

Case 2 – Appropriate referrals

During a check-up the dentist sees an ulcerated area under the tongue. The patient, who is 70, says it has been there for six weeks.

What action should the dentist take?

Any suspicious lesion should be investigated and the dentist should make arrangements for the patient to be seen by a maxillo-facial surgeon or a consultant in oral medicine for an opinion ensuring that the referral letter conveys the urgency of the case. The dentist should ensure that the patient has been seen in due course as referral letters can get lost and a delay in treatment can affect the long-term outcome. Importantly, dental professionals should ensure that they keep adequate records, including medical histories, and should facilitate patients if they seek access to their records. The GDC requires that dental professionals are responsible for 'putting patients' interests first and acting to protect them'. Putting patients' interests first means placing them before your own interests, and those of any colleague, organisation or business. Dental professionals should be aware of and comply with any complaints procedure that their practice operates. Dental professionals should only work within the limits of their knowledge, professional competence and physical abilities. The dental professional should always be willing to refer patients for a second opinion and seek further advice where it is necessary or if the patient requests it.

Case 3 – Access to records

A patient attends the practice requesting their records.

What should the practitioner do?

Under the Data Protection Act, a patient is entitled to copies of their records and radiographs and fee may be charged for this. There is a maximum fee set out in the Data Protection Act. Where the patient does not wish to pay for copying of radiographs, then it may be appropriate for the patient to ask their new dentist to write to the practitioner requesting a loan of the radiographs, accompanied by an authorisation from the patient. These radiographs should then be returned to the original practitioner.

Dental professionals should ensure that they are protected against claims at all times, including claims relating to a past period of practice, to enable patients to claim compensation where necessary.

Case 4 – Broken instrument

A practitioner is carrying out root canal treatment on the right first permanent molar and a file breaks.

What should she do?

The breakage of an endodontic instrument is, in itself, not negligent if the practitioner has been using the file in accordance with current teaching and practice and the lifespan of the file has not been exceeded. The patient should be advised of the problem and a decision taken about the appropriate treatment, which may be:

- removal by the practitioner
- completion of the root canal treatment
- referral to an endodontic specialist.

This should also be clearly noted in the records. A failure to advise the patient of the broken instrument would be criticised should this come to cause problems in the future and there would be the potential for a claim against the practitioner.

As a dental professional, if you believe your health, behaviour or professional performance or that of a colleague is affecting the care of patients, then you should seek advice from an appropriate colleague or professional organisation or from your defence organisation.

Case 5 – Whistle-blowing

You are an associate in general dental practice. Mr Davis, a dentist in his late fifties, has recently stopped working in a neighbouring practice and the practice has since closed down. Your practice principal had known Mr Davis for some years. A number of Mr Davis's former patients have now come to see you, and you are concerned at the level of untreated decay and periodontal disease.

What action would you take – as you are aware the practitioner is still continuing to work in another part of the county?

As an associate in general dental practice, you should actively consider contacting Mr Davis, either directly yourself or by asking your practice principal to do so. Alternatively, if Mr Davis is still working in the Health Service, then it may be appropriate to seek advice from the local dental adviser. Alternatively, contact with the local dental committee may be appropriate. Ultimately, it may be necessary for you to consider contacting the GDC if other routes do not prove successful.

Case 6 – Treating a minor

A 10-year-old boy attends your surgery on his own. He is complaining of toothache. He asks to be seen.

What would you do?

The dental care professional will have to consider whether they should be treating this child and to what extent. An attempt should be made to contact his parents or those with parental responsibility. If this is not possible, then a decision would have to be made as to whether the child was Gillick competent (see p. 41). If the dental care professional felt that the child was competent to consent to an examination, then this could be carried out. The practitioner himself will have to decide whether it is appropriate to carry out any further treatment. This will depend on the condition that the child is complaining of and the type of treatment that would be necessary for this condition. Any permanent treatment, such as an extraction, should only be considered as a last resort, and preferably would only be done following consultation with a colleague to confirm the necessity for the extraction and that it was in the best interests of the child. Ideally, only a reversible procedure should be carried out, such as a temporary dressing, if that was appropriate.

Ideally, the condition of the child's mouth should be assessed and then this communicated to those with parental responsibility, who should be asked to attend so that the treatment plan can be discussed and consent obtained.

Case 7 – Patient autonomy versus acting in the best interests of the patient

A 15-year-old attends a dental practitioner, together with her mother, requesting veneers on the upper lateral incisors (which are slightly out of line), as she wishes to start a modelling contract. The dentist examines the girl and identifies that orthodontic treatment may allow for alignment of the teeth without preparation of the teeth for veneers. The mother and the daughter are not prepared to wait two years for the orthodontic treatment to be completed. They insist on the veneers.

The practitioner has to decide whether to comply with their wishes. What should he do?

The practitioner will have to consider whether it is appropriate to treat these teeth with veneers on the basis of the patient's request for treatment. If, in the future, there were problems with these teeth, then there is the potential for the practitioner to be called to justify his decision.

It is important to understand the patient's expectations of treatment; the gap between the patient's expectations and the dentist's or dental professional's ability to deliver the treatment can be a cause for complaints or potentially a claim where the treatment does not go according to plan. A dental professional should not carry out treatment which they believe not to be in the patient's best interests; the patient is always at liberty to seek a second opinion, and the dental professional may help them to do so if requested.

Case 8 – Treatment planning

A patient attends requesting the replacement of their upper central and lateral incisors by a bridge. The patient is currently wearing a denture and the periodontal condition of the maxillary canines is questionable. The practitioner takes appropriate radiographs and advises the patient that the upper canines are not ideal abutments for a bridge and the long-term future prognosis is not good. The patient insists on having the treatment done.

What should the practitioner do?

If the practitioner considers that the treatment is inappropriate, it should not be carried out. The practitioner is the professional with specialist knowledge and training, and even if the patient were to sign a disclaimer, that disclaimer would potentially damage his or her defence. A practitioner should never carry out treatment which they believe is inappropriate and not in the patient's best interests. Patients always have the right to seek a second opinion, as discussed in the preceding case. In Chapter 5 we looked at the principle of autonomy and it is worth remembering that dental professionals also have autonomy; when others seek to infringe this inappropriately (whether colleagues, patients or patients' relatives), the dental professional does not have any duty to collude with them.

Case 9 – Providing estimates

A patient attends for an examination as a new patient. The dentist identifies that extensive crown and bridge work are required. Following discussions, they verbally agree a treatment plan and the practitioner believes he told the patient how much each crown would cost but did not give her a written estimate. During the course of the treatment, the patient does not pay any fees. At the end of treatment, the patient is sent a bill for £2500. When the patient receives this bill, she writes a letter of complaint saying that although she was happy with the treatment, she had only anticipated a bill for £350 as this is what her friend had paid for her treatment under the NHS. What should the practitioner do?

The dentist in this case has two potential problems. First, was the patient expecting this treatment under the NHS, and, second, who will be believed in relation to the discussions surrounding the cost of treatment? The GDC's guidance says patients should be given full information 'so that they can make decisions ... giving full information on proposed treatment and possible costs'. The practitioner will have to decide whether to pursue the patient for the full amount through the courts if necessary, risk losing the claim and potentially have a complaint made against them to the GDC.

It is vitally important for patients to understand whether treatment is to be given privately or under the NHS, and patients should always be given details of the charges for an initial consultation. In order to avoid misunderstandings, patients should always be given a treatment plan and an estimate of the costs. Ideally this should be in written form. Should any amendments be necessary, these amendments should be given to the patient before treatment is continued. A signature on an estimate or treatment plan is not worth the paper it is written on if a patient has not fully understood what the proposed treatment is. Always ensure that the patient understands that they are able to change their mind and that they can ask questions at any time. All members of the dental team will be involved in the treatment of patients and should be able to respond to patients' requests for further information either themselves or by referral to a colleague.

Treatment plans and estimates should be given in line with GDC requirements and whether the patient is to be treated under the NHS in line with NHS regulations. Patients have a right to refuse treatment and during the consenting process patients should be made aware of the option of having no treatment and the likely risks that that would entail.

The question of who can actually give consent can cause dental professionals problems but, in general, every adult has the right to make their own decisions and it must be assumed that they are able to do so unless they demonstrate otherwise. It is the responsibility of the dental professional to assess whether the patient is able to give informed consent and whether they are capable of weighing up the pros and cons of any particular procedure. Dental professionals should consult their defence organisation if in any doubt.

Case 10 – Dental reference officers

Patients being treated under the new NHS General Dental Service (nGDS) contract have to sign a form and in that form the patient gives their consent to their records being looked at by a dental reference officer (DRO).

How do I deal with this?

Often patients will sign the form put in front of them by the receptionist without reading it in detail. Therefore they may not be aware that their records may be looked at by a DRO as part of the monitoring of NHS practices. In the UK, the DRO is an experienced dental practitioner employed by the Dental Reference Service of the Dental Practice Board for England and Wales, or the Scottish Dental Reference Service (part of NHS Scotland), and his or her role is to examine patients who have been treated and to review records to see if they are of an acceptable standard. In a busy NHS practice it may be impractical for the receptionist to highlight this paragraph but ideally it should be done. As a back-up there should be a notice in the waiting room advising the patient of this paragraph and consideration should also be given to it in the patient information leaflet. The GDC sets out the principles of patient confidentiality in a separate booklet – *Principles of Confidentiality* – and in *Standards for Dental Professionals* it refers to this booklet. It is important to ensure that all members of the dental team understand the need for confidentiality. In most cases there will be a confidentiality clause in the dental professional's contract. It is also important to remember that information should be kept confidential even after the death of a patient.

All dental professionals should understand that information should only be shared with colleagues when it is necessary and in the patient's best interests. Patients do have the right to withhold permission for dental professionals to share information about them with others. It is important for patients to understand what purpose the disclosure of information serves, and this will be especially true where photographs or data relating to patients are used for teaching or other educational purposes (see Chapter 5).

It is vitally important that patients' confidential information is not released accidentally and dental professionals should always ensure that they do not talk about patients where they can be overheard. This can be a very real problem in dental teaching hospitals or clinics where there are several chairs in one room. Patients' records – whether they are paper or computer-based – should be stored securely, and protocols should be in place to ensure that records are not lost. Within the confines of a dental practice it can sometimes be difficult for patients to discuss matters of a confidential nature easily. Dental professionals should ensure that patients are able to discuss confidential information in an area where they cannot be overheard.

There may be situations in which dental professionals are expected to disclose confidential information in the 'public interest'. Before doing so, dental professionals should seek advice from their defence organisation. Instances in which it may be appropriate to release information include when there has been a serious crime or when the conduct of a patient may lead other people to be placed in danger. Before disclosing information the patient's consent should be requested but if they refuse or it is impractical to do so then advice should be sought. A dental professional may also receive a court order to release patient information without their consent, but only the minimum amount of information should be disclosed. Dental professionals may be required to justify and explain why they disclosed that information.

Case 11 – Dealing with the police

A practitioner has a call from the police asking for the records of a patient.

What should she do?

The practitioner should ascertain why the police wish to see the records. There may be good reasons for the practitioner to allow the police to see the records, such as when a dead body has been discovered and the dental records would assist in the identification of that body. However, if they are seeking the records purely to try to identify a person, then it may be appropriate for them to seek a court order to obtain those records.

The police might also attend with an appointment card and ask which patient it relates to. Again, the practitioner should attempt to identify the seriousness of the offence to which it relates and consider consulting their defence organisation for advice. If it is deemed appropriate to give that information, then only the minimum amount of information should be provided.

Practitioners have sometimes been asked for records of missing patients where there is no body. Usually, disclosure would be resisted as without a body the records are of no use. In some jurisdictions, when a person is missing and there is a high suspicion that they have been killed, requests for copy notes and radiographs may be received. In these circumstances disclosure may be appropriate but advice should be obtained from the defence organisation.

Confidentiality checklist:

- Who wants to know?
- Why do they want to know?
- Are they entitled to know?
- Has the patient given their consent?

Case 12 – Emergency/third-person presence

You are a general dental practitioner. You receive an out-of-hours call to see a patient with toothache. Unfortunately, you are unable to get your dental nurse or other member of staff to attend.

What should you do?

You will obviously wish to consider whether it is appropriate for you to see the patient alone. The GDC's guidance says:

> 'There may be circumstances in which it is not possible for a trained person to be present – for example, if you are treating a patient in an out-of-hours emergency or on a home visit. If this is the case, you are responsible for assessing the possible risk of continuing with treatment in the absence of a trained person.'

It may be appropriate for the practitioner to ask the patient to bring a third person with him or her. You will have to consider whether it is appropriate for you to carry out any operative treatment if you do not have adequate support. You would also have to bear in mind that there should be a medical emergency, would you be able to deal with it? How would you defend yourself against a spurious complaint of sexual assault in such circumstances? Remember, this kind of complaint need not only be made by a member of the opposite sex, but could be made by someone of your own gender.

Co-operating with other members of the dental team and other healthcare colleagues in the interests of patients

In many instances the treatment of patients will require the co-operation of more than one member of the dental team. It is important that all team members respect the role of their colleagues in the treatment of patients, and recognise that there should be effective communication and sharing of knowledge with other members of the dental team. Usually, when treating patients there should be someone else – preferably a registered dental professional – present in the room, who is trained to deal with medical emergencies. However, there may be exceptional circumstances in which it is not possible for a trained person to be present.

It is an NHS requirement that a fully equipped and operational crash trolley or resuscitation kit should be available in every dental practice or clinic.

Case 13 – Permitted duties

You are a new associate at a general dental practice; during your first morning at work there, the principal tells you that all the patients who are new to the practice have an orthopantomogram when they arrive and that this will be taken by the nurse.

What would you consider doing in this situation?

There are two main issues to consider here. First, no radiographic image should be taken without the patient being examined and a radiograph being prescribed, and the radiograph being taken should be appropriate for the clinical situation. Second, the associate should find out whether the dental nurse has received appropriate training to be taking radiographs. If radiographs are to be taken, then the associate should ensure that they are only taken following his prescription and that the nurse should only take them if they have been trained. It is important that dental professionals only carry out those duties which they are allowed to perform and for which they have been trained. All members of the dental team are individually responsible and accountable for their own actions and for the treatment and procedures that they perform.

Case 14 – Obtaining a medical history

A patient has been referred to a hygienist/therapist for scaling. On questioning, the patient tells the hygienist/therapist that they have a heart defect and that they usually have antibiotic cover. The hygienist/therapist contacts the dentist, who says: 'Just do a superficial scale and polish.'

What should the hygienist/therapist do?

If it has been ascertained that the patient requires antibiotic cover before dental treatment, then this should be given. If the patient has not received a prescription and the dentist is suggesting that a superficial scale and polish is carried out, then the hygienist should not carry out the treatment as it would be inappropriate to do so and she or he would face the risk of either a claim should subacute bacterial endocarditis develop or potential referral to the GDC.

The GDC states in Standards for Dental Professionals that all dental professionals should 'treat patients fairly and in line with the law', and that they should 'not discriminate against patients because of their sex, age, race, ethnic origin, nationality, special needs, or disability, sexuality, health, lifestyle, beliefs or any other relevant consideration.'

Maintaining your professional knowledge and competence

All dental professionals should ensure that they register with the GDC or their own professional body and that they actively participate in continuing professional development (CPD). They should ensure that they comply with the requirements for CPD as set out by their registration body and that they are able to demonstrate their attendance at appropriate courses. Patients should always be treated in line with current teaching and practice and dental professionals should be aware of the laws and regulations which affect their work premises and ensure that they are followed.

Case 15 – Health and safety

You have just started work in a new practice under the nGDS contract and you find that you have only two high-speed hand-pieces. Your dental nurse tells you that the principal of the practice says just to wipe them over if there is no time to sterilise them. What should you do?

As a registered dental professional in general dental practice you are ultimately responsible for your infection control procedures. You should practise in accordance with guidance set out by the Department of Health, the British Dental Association – or other professional body – and the primary care trust. You will be held responsible by the GDC if there is a complaint. Once dental nurses are registered, they will also be accountable to the GDC and their registration could also be at risk.

Case 16 – Consent in general dental practice and patients with learning difficulties or special needs

Charlie is a 17-year-old boy with learning difficulties and epilepsy. He lives at home with his elderly widowed mother who has arthritis, which is making her increasingly housebound. His mother has brought Charlie to your practice in the past, but he is an irregular attender. He presents to your practice one lunchtime, unaccompanied, complaining that he has just fallen over and broken a front tooth. On examination you note that a maxillary central incisor is fractured subgingivally and needs to be extracted.

What should you do?

The GDC Standards Guidance on consent states that the main ethical principles are:

- informed consent
- voluntary decision making
- ability.

It is not enough that you tell Charlie about the proposed treatment – it needs to be presented in a way that he can understand, he should be given the opportunity to ask questions, and you should be satisfied that he understands what you have told him and can weigh the information needed to make a decision. There are four issues that need to be considered here are:

- his age
- his learning difficulty
- his infirm mother
- telephone consent.

Age

Technically Charlie is still a minor. The Gillick case (see Chapter 5) established that children under 16 years can give consent if the practitioner believes that they have the capacity to understand the implications of the proposed treatment. For those with impaired capacity the limit is 18 years. This takes us to the second issue.

Learning difficulty

This requires a judgement by the practitioner on the extent of the learning difficulty. If there is a medical report that suggests that Charlie has a mental age of, say, 8 years, then it is probably not appropriate to assume that he has the ability to fully understand. If this is the case, we come to the third issue.

Infirm mother

Ideally you would like his mother to attend the surgery so that you can explain the situation to her and obtain her consent (as well as Charlie's). However, it is impractical for her to leave the house and attend your surgery at such short notice. Note, however, that once Charlie becomes 18 years old no adult can give consent on his behalf until the Mental Capacity Act comes into effect in April 2007.

Is telephone consent satisfactory?

For an irreversible procedure such as extraction, ideally Charlie's mother should be present to give her consent. It might be reasonable to place a temporary dressing in the tooth to alleviate the pain until such time as he can be accompanied by his mother. If this is out of the question, then telephone consent, together with a second opinion from another registered dental practitioner should be the way forward. This must be clearly and fully recorded in his notes, and signed by both dentists.

Case 17 – Consent in oral surgery

You are an oral surgery house officer and are called to see 4-year-old Kylie, who has been hit a glancing blow to the face by a playground swing. Kylie has a facial laceration that requires suturing, but no other injuries. You know that, if properly managed, the wound will heal with almost no scar. She is clearly distressed, crying throughout your examination, but has been basically co-operative; her mother is also distressed, but is coping with the situation. You obtain consent from the mother to place the sutures. However, when you start to explain to Kylie she cries even more and climbs onto her mother's lap and clings to her neck. You suggest that the sutures are placed under a short general anaesthetic, but Kylie's mother says that she does not want Kylie to have that.

What should you do?

Kylie's behaviour suggests that she has not consented to the sutures. However, she is too young and distressed to understand the implications of not treating the wound. A general anaesthetic has been excluded by her mother's wishes. Sedation, either as inhalation sedation or by pharmacological means is a possibility, but she may still resist.

Restraint is a further option, but is a grey area from a medico-legal point of view. If you wish to use restraint (eg wrapping in a blanket, or the use of a 'papoose board') you must be sure that the mother fully understand the procedure, that she consents to the procedure, and, preferably, that she will assist with the restraint (thereby providing implied consent to the procedure). You must be fully aware of both the task in hand for Kylie, and also be sensitive to her mother's mood.

If it all becomes too much for the mother, it must be your professional judgement that dictates which approach you adopt with the mother at this point. You should discuss with her whether she is still happy for you to proceed in her absence. If so, it is prudent that you have nursing assistance throughout the procedure, and the nurse witnesses the mother's consent. If you feel that she will not be happy being separated from her child for the remainder of the procedure, then it is wise to stop and discuss future management with the mother (probably having to persuade her that a general anaesthetic is the only remaining option). At the end of the procedure, ensure that you have a full and clear written record in the file of all the circumstances and outcome.

The mother is within her rights to withdraw consent at any time (the relevant wording from the GDC guidelines is given below). Here you are dealing primarily with the mother rather than the patient. The GDC guidance is that:

- Giving and getting consent is a process, not a one-off event. It should be part of an ongoing discussion between you and the patient.

- Once a patient has given consent, they may withdraw it at any time, including during the procedure.

- Make sure you know how much authority they have given you. For example, be aware of whether the patient agrees to all or part of a proposed treatment plan.

Note: In medicine children rarely co-operate with procedures such as inoculations against contagious diseases, but this is carried out in spite of their protests, and usually without written parental consent.

Dental professionals' problem page

I am a vocational dental practitioner. What should I do if a 14 year old female patient, her parent or guardian expresses concern about the way she, the patient, has been treated by her previous dentist? For example, what if she alleges inappropriate contact by the dentist – this might include the dentist sending her suggestive messages by text or phone – or inappropriate touching while she was in the dental chair?

If you have concerns about the way in which young and/or vulnerable patients under the age of 18 have been treated, remember that child protection procedures should be in place in every dental practice, clinic and hospital. You and all other dental professionals should understand how to access these procedures and what to do in the event of a complaint or if you believe action needs to be taken. Your dental defence organisation should be able to offer advice. The GDC provides guidance in *Standards for Dental Professionals*. It is important to remember that you have a duty to act where appropriate. It is also advisable to be discreet in dealing with this matter; it is possible that the allegations are spurious, with no basis in reality. If you were to be indiscreet in relaying the accusations about the other dentist to those with no need to become involved, and these allegations were subsequently found to be without foundation, you could find yourself facing a lawsuit for defamation or a complaint to the GDC for unprofessional conduct. It is not acceptable to do nothing when such an allegation is made; inaction could amount to professional negligence.

I am a 22-year-old dental student in my final year at dental school. A 21-year-old female patient I have been treating for the past four months at the adult dental health clinic in my dental hospital has just asked me out for a drink, making it clear that it might not just be a drink that is on offer. I am attracted to her and would like to take up the invitation. What should I do?

Dental professionals should be aware of the appropriate boundaries in their relationships with patients and should not abuse these relationships. Your patient is unlikely to distinguish between a student and a qualified dentist; the ethical requirement for a qualified dentist to avoid developing an intimate relationship with his or her patients could equally be said to apply to you therefore (same sex relationships are included in this guidance). If you will no longer be treating this patient from this point on, it might be acceptable for you to agree to meeting socially, with the proviso that – should the patient present in the dental hospital again – she should be treated by someone other than you. The same applies in general practice; it is generally seen as a bad thing for a dentist or dental professional to develop a reputation for going out with his or her patients – if 'going out' is merely a euphemism for having an intimate or sexual relationship on each occasion. The reality is that – especially in more rural areas – some of your patients will become your friends, and it is therefore difficult to be too proscriptive when it comes to accepting social invitations to dinner, etc.

What should I do if a patient offers me a 'thank you' gift?

Again, it depends on the situation and the patient. It is inevitable that some patients will want to express their appreciation to their dentist or dental care professional, for example at Christmas, or when the dental professional has provided service over and above the call of duty. However, dental professionals should never accept a gift which may affect their referral – or which may be given as a result of the referral – as this may appear to affect their professional judgement. Discretion and common sense should be applied. A bottle of wine or a box of chocolates are obviously rather different types of present to a brown envelope full of bank notes!

I am a hygienist. I have heard the other hygienist in the practice where I work in conversation with her patients. She claims to be able to perform procedures which are currently restricted to dentists. When I challenged her about this, she said the practice principal allows her to do so 'on the quiet', because she is so competent. Is this permissible?

Practitioners should not make any misleading claims about their abilities, their training or qualifications, or the likely success of a treatment. All dental professionals need to be aware of their limitations, both legally and clinically. The GDC has the ability to strike off from the Dental Register a practitioner who exceeds their permitted responsibilities, or indeed a dentist who instructs or permits a dental care professional to do so in his or her practice (eg a general dental practitioner who uses nurses as unqualified hygienists). A case of professional misconduct recently heard by the GDC in 2006 led to the erasure from the Register of a dentist who permitted her completely untrained and unqualified boyfriend to present himself as a dentist and to treat unsuspecting patients within the dental practice, subjecting them to an unnecessary and painful experience. In such circumstances, consent to treatment cannot be valid (where a person has misrepresented him- or herself as dentally qualified) and thus such behaviour may very well constitute an assault (an offence in criminal law for which the offender is liable on conviction to a fine and/or a prison sentence) and/or a battery (a civil tort or wrong, for which the offender can be sued in civil law, usually for the payment of damages).

The cases and problems detailed above have been broad in their scope, covering a range of dilemmas facing dental professionals in a variety of situations; most of these have been to do with patients. In the next chapter, we go on to look at the ethical, legal and professional challenges that might occur within the dental team.

CHAPTER 7
ETHICS OF TEAMWORKING IN PRACTICE

CHAPTER 7
ETHICS OF TEAMWORKING IN PRACTICE

Ethical teamwork – leading and managing a team; dealing with conflicts

Dental ethics, leadership and management might not seem to have an obvious link. But – as we have previously noted – ethics is about much more than following rules and applying regulations; it is about behaviour and actions, the ways in which one responds to diverse situations and challenges. An ethical approach is essential if the leadership of a dental team in general practice or in hospital is to be truly effective. Leadership of a dental team is about more than management:

- it implies the ability to inspire trust and loyalty among colleagues.

- It demands that potentially damaging behaviour is confronted and dealt with in an appropriate way.

- It requires the practice of kindness, compassion and consideration for one another.

Below we provide a variety of challenging scenarios, with some suggestions on how each might be dealt with. You may find it helpful to use these scenarios as a stimulus for a small-group discussion or in a team meeting, as a way of confronting – indirectly – dysfunctional behaviour in one or more of the team members. You might choose to use the scenarios in a prophylactic way – in order to avoid a similar situation arising in your own setting. We have deliberately made some of the scenarios complex, embodying a combination of common problems encountered in dental teams. All of these scenarios have been tried and tested around the UK in the education and training of dental professionals, and are based on real-life situations which we have either encountered ourselves or have heard about from colleagues working in general dental practice, specialist practice, the community dental service or the hospital dental service. If the scenarios are to be used with several small groups of students or trainees, or with qualified staff in practice, community clinics or hospitals, we suggest the following approach:

1 Divide participants into small groups of six to eight. Ideally, the group should be seated in a circle or horseshoe shape, with the facilitator at the head of the group. In a lecture theatre setting, these are commonly known as 'buzz groups', formed by getting sets of students in adjacent rows to turn around and face each other.

2 Appoint either an experienced teacher, clinical or non-clinical, as the group facilitator, or a student/trainee/staff member as chair for each group. His or her role is to keep the group on task, ensure that all members participate and contribute, and to provide guidance as appropriate; a facilitator is not expected to provide all the answers – this is the group's task.

3 Invite each small group to appoint a rapporteur who will report their conclusions back to the plenary (large) group, and a scribe who will write a summary of the group's discussions on a flip chart or whiteboard, or record these on paper or a laptop.

4 Appoint a timekeeper for each small group whose task it is to provide time checks and to remind their colleagues when they are approaching the end of the session.

5 After a period of time (say, 15 minutes per scenario), the rapporteur for each group should report its discussions and conclusions to the plenary or large group.

A – The under-confident but competent dentist

Your vocational dental practitioner (VDP), Jan, is in her first month in your training practice. She has asked to see you at lunchtime to discuss some of her concerns. In essence she is worried because she feels that she is meeting many new clinical situations and is struggling to cope with them as well as she feels she should be able to. She was always near the top of the class at dental school, but is now wondering if it is all too much for her and whether she should have chosen a different career altogether.

Background information

Jan is actually perfectly competent – if a little slow still. She takes her time when making clinical decisions because she is thinking through all the options and wants to be sure that she is making the right choice. She is getting on well with both patients and practice staff. You have observed Jan performing several procedures now, and are satisfied that she is safe. You would like to boost her confidence.

What should you do?

Patients often say that they appreciate the time and depth of explanation that they get when they see a VDP. Lack of communication or insufficient attention to obtaining a valid and informed consent are often the reasons why a complaint or claim is instigated, and this is unlikely to be a problem for Jan when dealing with her patients. It is obviously better to be cautious than reckless as a dental professional, but one of the aims of vocational training (VT) is to give the new dental graduate an opportunity to develop in a protected environment. We all need praise and reassurance and it would be helpful for the other members of the practice who work with Jan to give her feedback on their view of how she deals with patients. It might also be appropriate for Jan to do a patient satisfaction survey and audit the results. This could be run in conjunction with the rest of the practice. The trainer could use some of the tutorial time to look at various patients whose treatment she has planned. Both Jan and her trainer's patients could be peer reviewed. The trainer may try to agree some targets for Jan to try to meet over a period of time to see if her operating speed can be increased.

In essence, Jan needs to be encouraged and helped to appreciate that she is competent. This can be achieved by observing her in practice and then asking her to focus on a clinical event, using a process known as 'positive critique'. For example, after having seen Jan perform a root canal treatment, once the patient has left the room, the trainer asks Jan to describe how the procedure went. Firstly, the trainer asks her to tell him what went well, then to tell him what could be improved or done differently next time. On each occasion, the trainer should provide his own constructive comments and feedback.

B – The arrogant young dentist

Your VDP, Jason, is in the sixth month of vocational training. He really wonders why he needs to attend the day/block release course for the VT scheme, and thinks the tutorials with you are probably unnecessary (though he thinks you could benefit from listening to some of his ideas about dentistry). He is looking forward to putting up his brass plate outside his own practice, but wishes he didn't have to put up with the restrictive rules of NHS dentistry, such irritating patients, older dentists and other practice staff.

Background information

You are an experienced trainer. Your VDP, Jason, is a living nightmare. He has all the confidence in the world (that's why you offered him the post at interview) but little competence – despite increasingly frequent constructive feedback from you. If anything, since qualification, his clinical skills have deteriorated as his speed has increased. The practice staff are up in arms over his arrogant behaviour and you have had several complaints from patients. He seems completely impervious to the poor quality of his own work and the effect his abrasive manner has on other people. He has told you in the past that his ambition is to pay off his student debt, buy a house and pay cash for an expensive sports car within the first year of owning his own practice.

What should you do?

Consider the reasons why Jason is behaving like this. Does he equate money with a successful practice? Is he in competition with his erstwhile student colleagues? Is his arrogance such that he has no insight into his own behaviour? Has he emerged from dental school believing that he has all the knowledge and skills required to provide comprehensive dental care for each of his patients? Understanding the motivation for his behaviour will help you to address the problem. While you could argue that his ambition is not your concern, it is certainly your concern that he is upsetting both your staff members and your patients. Ambition in the newly qualified is normal and to be encouraged, but Jason's ambition is disproportionate and, as will be discussed in Chapter 8, you have a wider responsibility to the dental profession to attempt a change of attitude in your trainee. Key aims of vocational training are:

1   To enable trainees to practice and improve their skills.

2   To introduce trainees to all aspects of general dental practice.

3   To identify a trainee's strengths and weaknesses and balance them through a planned programme of training.

4   To promote oral health and good-quality dental care for patients.

5   To develop further and implement peer- and self-review, and to promote awareness of the need for professional education, training and audit as a continuing process.

Jason is clearly failing to achieve points 1, 3, 4, and 5. The trainer has three main roles:

- To interact with the trainee to provide tuition, advice, information and facilities to fulfil the aims and objectives of training so that the postgraduate dental dean may issue a certificate of completion of vocational training.

- To prepare for the role of trainer by acquiring knowledge of the educational processes and interpersonal skills necessary and by learning how to apply them in the general dental practice setting.

- To liaise with the VT adviser, the regional adviser and the postgraduate dental dean as necessary to ensure that the trainee completes their training.

Your role as a trainer is to assist your trainee and, under the circumstances described above, will be to identify their personal strengths and weaknesses, and promote high-quality dental care. Having reached the halfway mark in the training year, you have a limited amount of time in which to get your trainee to identify their weaknesses, agree a development programme and monitor the effectiveness of the programme. You will need to set aside time to discuss the issues with your trainee. You should describe the problems that have been identified, specifying incidents in support of your concern, in a non-confrontational manner. Help Jason to understand why his behaviour is unacceptable, and give him the opportunity to develop his own plans to modify his behaviour. You should help with this task, making sure that he is setting himself clear, reasonable and achievable goals, with an obvious means of showing that the goals have been achieved within a reasonable timescale. This should be recorded, with signed copies kept by yourself and by Jason. Hopefully this will lead to a change in Jason. However, if the problems persist, and you as his trainer feel that it is beyond your skills to help Jason, then you have the dental postgraduate vocational adviser and/or regional adviser to turn to for further assistance.

C – Staff with personal problems

Seema, a dental hygienist, is in her fourth month in the practice of which you are the practice manager. She gets on well with you, the other practice staff, and the patients, and feels she has been doing quite well. However, her elderly father (76 years old) had a severe stroke last month and is now bedridden. Seema's mother (75 years old) suffers from heart disease and is finding it difficult to cope with the effort of caring for her husband. Seema has a brother who lives in the USA with his wife and family and who thinks that it is her responsibility to look after their father. Her parents live 200 miles away, and the strain of worrying about the family is having a profound effect on her.

Background information

You are an experienced practice manager. You have noticed over the past four weeks that Seema has become very withdrawn and uncommunicative. You want to help if there is a problem, but are not quite sure how to do so as she has not responded yet to your invitations to talk about whatever it is that is bothering her.

What should you do?

Seema is clearly under a lot of pressure. She is in a new job which she likes and doesn't want to let her new employers down. She has elderly and infirm parents who she wants to care for, but the distance makes anything other than a weekend trip impossible. Finally, she has a brother who is adding to her feelings of guilt by expecting her to be responsible for looking after their parents' health. All this would be a challenge for anyone to cope with.

As practice manager, all you know is that things are not well with Seema. You need to agree a time with Seema where you can discuss the situation. Holding the meeting in a location that is 'neutral ground' may help, together with an assurance that the meeting is nothing to do with the quality or quantity of her work, and perhaps turning the situation around and suggesting that all new employees are given the opportunity to give feedback to yourself regarding the practice and how it runs, with a view to improving the service. You can prepare for the meeting by seeking information from other practice members to see if they are aware of any particular problems that Seema has. Assuming that the meeting with Seema is successful in getting her to tell you her problems, you then need to help her reach a solution. Allowing her time to spend time with her parents to arrange with the local doctor and social services the homecare that her parents clearly need should assuage her concerns to an extent. You will then need to arrange further informal meetings with Seema to ensure that she is coping with the situation. If the situation is not resolving, you could assist Seema in seeking a job that is close to her parents' home.

D – The financially challenged dental therapist

Sally, a newly qualified dental therapist, is in her second month in the practice. She is experiencing serious financial difficulties and is currently trying to juggle a sizeable student debt, a hefty car loan and a mortgage. She has already borrowed more to try to consolidate her debts but this has just increased her anxiety. This is all causing her performance at work to suffer badly; she is snappy with practice staff and patients, tires easily, and finds it hard to concentrate. Her family never talked about money, and she is deeply embarrassed at being in this situation.

Background information

You are a fairly experienced practice owner. You are aware that Sally is under-performing but are not sure why. Your attempts to elicit the reasons from her have met with a denial that there is a problem.

What should you do?

Sally is clearly not managing and the pressure she is under is affecting the care of your patients and the stability of the practice team. If financial problems are not dealt with early they will inevitably lead to more serious problems and it is essential the issues are addressed and dealt with promptly, however difficult it might be to discuss the subject. The issues are unlikely to be resolved unless Sally is given support and guidance as newly qualified members of the dental team often find the balance between business and health difficult to comprehend.

Regular opportunities to review the progress of your staff and their contribution to the team are essential and this is particularly relevant to newly qualified therapists who will have limited knowledge of managing the financial impact of working in a general practice environment. As an experienced professional and team leader you should arrange regular private meetings to review progress and identify any problem areas.

Once you have explained the purpose of these routine discussions it will be important to ensure Sally understands you realise how difficult the transition to the working environment can be and how anyone who is newly qualified undoubtedly will be having issues with managing financially. She must be reassured that it is vitally important to resolve any problems before they become insurmountable, and that you will be happy to discuss any issues confidentially with a view to helping her find a solution. In view of the observations from other team members about her professional attitude, it is also important to explain sensitively the concerns within the practice about her behaviour, but ensure she understands you are confident that between you the situation will improve if you can find a way of helping her. You will need to decide how to handle the staff situation and agree whether Sally would prefer to quietly explain to colleagues that she has been under pressure or whether you should speak to the team yourself to explain that you are aware of their concerns and would appreciate their support and understanding while you are trying to resolve the problems with Sally.

Dividing the problem into the different component parts should make the problem feel more manageable and it may be that she can be persuaded to speak to her parents, arrange an appointment with a financial adviser, or even discuss a temporary change in working hours until she feels more able to cope. Setting a timescale for a resolution is essential and you may advise a transfer to a less stressful salaried working environment if the situation does not improve or resolve. If Sally persists in denying there are problems and your practice manager is also unable to communicate with her, it may be necessary to explain your concerns and ask her to leave.

E – The over-cautious dental hospital trainee

Anil, a dental senior house officer (SHO) in his third month of the local general professional training programme, is currently working in your clinic in the dental hospital. He is meticulous to the point of obsession in caring for his patients, desperately worried that he might miss something important when he makes a diagnosis (over-prescribing, in your view, several diagnostic procedures such as radiographs) or that his work might fall short of perfection when he performs even the simplest procedure. This, after all, was how he was taught at dental school. This means that he found it very difficult to cope with life as a VDP in general dental practice and was hoping that a return to a dental hospital environment would restore the feeling of security he had as a dental student. He badly wants to get onto the specialist training course in your department.

Background information

You are a newly appointed hospital consultant. Your fellow consultants, associate specialists, and the clinic staff have asked you to speak to your SHO, Anil. There is widespread concern that he is far too slow in treating patients. In particular, his regular nurse is getting annoyed at often having to work through lunch and work past her official going-home time and the radiography department is concerned about the number of radiographs that he requests. You believe Anil to be a competent dentist, despite his obsessive attention to detail, and want to ensure you don't lose him from the clinic and the specialty.

What should you do?

Anil's caution is laudable, but impractical. He needs to develop more self-confidence and, from the story given above, it is unlikely that he will become over-confident in the near future. In this situation the 'apprentice' style of education is inappropriate. Expecting Anil to improve just by being in a hospital environment is unrealistic, and may even be counter-productive when he compares his skills with those of his peers, and he may even be demoralised by the skills demonstrated by more senior staff members.

The issue of over-prescription of investigative tests may be addressed by an audit project, in which even the discussion of an appropriate 'gold standard' (see Chapter 9) will help Anil to understand that he is not conforming to acceptable practice.

His slow speed in treating patients may be due to poor time management, eg not realising how long a task will take him. You need to make a judgement on how to manage this. the choice is to continue as before and urge him to accelerate, give him simpler tasks to undertake, or to book in fewer patients. In the longer term the latter approach may lead to problems with your waiting lists, and simpler tasks will not develop his clinical skills, although in the short term this might be a solution.

A discussion with Anil regarding your concerns must take place. This should be in a supportive manner, giving him the chance to explain his reasons for performing the way he does, and giving you the chance to express your concerns about his progress. You might wish to develop an 'action plan' in which you agree to arrange for help that is identified as a need between you.

F – The problematic student therapist

Rachel is a student therapist in your dental hospital. She has been overheard – and has been reported to you for – making disparaging comments about dentists, dental students and hygienists. She has told the other students that she used to do a lot of clinical work for her dentist when she was in practice, and that tutors make an unnecessary fuss about checking medical histories. Supervising staff have complained at the regular student progress reviews that her cross-infection control procedures are inadequate despite constant supervision and that she has claimed to have completed work that has not been done. She has also forged the signature of one of the dental therapy supervisors who is required to check and sign off her work in the clinic and is consistently being reprimanded for not checking the medical history before commencing invasive treatments.

Background information

You are the Principal Therapy Tutor in the dental care professional education and training centre, based in the dental school and hospital. Rachel had applied unsuccessfully to become a dental student, having worked as a dental nurse for five years in a specialist practice. She was subsequently accepted for training as a dental therapist, but has caused concern since the start of the course, not least for her attitude to tutors and clinical staff, as well as towards her fellow students.

What should you do?

The issues are extremely worrying as Rachel is clearly displaying totally unprofessional behaviour and does not yet appear to understand the roles and responsibilities of dental professionals. A number of the reported concerns would have led to disciplinary action for a qualified dental professional and there is no way this student should be permitted to continue to be registered as a student unless the issues are resolved. Rachel should be formally interviewed by the Principal Tutor in the presence of her personal tutor to ascertain the student's version of events. Following documentation of the meeting (signed and witnessed by all present), she should also be formally interviewed by appropriate academic representatives and provided with an action plan, counselling and individual supervision, or suspended pending further investigation and possible exclusion from the course.

G – The illegal denturist

Keith is a dental technician who works in your practice. One of the practice nurses shows you an advertisement in the local newspaper which says 'DISCOUNT DENTURES – have your dentures made, repaired, replaced and fitted by an experienced dental care professional. Call 07911 222101'. The number belongs to Keith's mobile phone. Further investigations reveal that he has set up what appears to be a backstreet practice in the town, where he is seeing patients, taking impressions and waxing up dentures, which he processes overnight and then fits in the patient's mouth the following day. You also discover, by accident, that the elderly mother of David, one of your patients, has been going to see him for her new dentures; David then tells you that, although his mother is not entirely happy with the colour of her new teeth, she doesn't want to complain as she felt she got a 'good service' from Keith (she says it was both cheap and quick), and because he is 'such a nice man'.

Background information

You are the dental practice owner. Keith has worked in the practice, which has a basement dental laboratory and a dental technician contract with several neighbouring practices, for several years. He is generally popular with the practice staff and his work is highly regarded by you and your fellow dentists.

What should you do?

Ethical – whistle-blowing

If the technician is not a registered dental care professional, then the practitioner has to consider whether he has a duty to advise the GDC of the clinical activities of the technician. It will be up to the GDC to decide what action to take. If he fails to inform the GDC, the practitioner may be considered to be 'covering', ie condoning the illegal activity of the technician.

Business/commercial aspects

The practitioner will have to consider the nature of the business relationship between the practitioner and the technician. Is he an employee, or a subcontractor and self-employed? He will also have to consider whether he will advise the other dentists. He should ask himself if the technician is aware of the regulations, and whether he can be made to reconsider his activities.

It is worth noting that this is an area of dental practice which has been controversial for many years, although there are a number of current developments in the UK which will provide the new GDC category of registered practitioners, the clinical dental technicians, with greater autonomy and opportunity for professional progression. Registration in this category will only be possible for those who have undertaken a satisfactory course of training, and have been able to demonstrate competence in a range of domains. In their current guidance regarding illegal practice and dental technicians, the GDC says (www.gdc-uk.org/Search+our+registers/Illegal+practice):

> 'The Dentists Act 1984 defines the practice of dentistry as "any such treatment, advice or attendance as is usually performed or given by dentists". It also includes any treatment or advice "in connection with the fitting, insertion or fixing of dentures, artificial teeth or other dental appliances".
>
> Currently in the UK it is illegal for an unregistered person (for example, a dental technician) to carry out work in the mouth of a patient. This could include taking an impression of the mouth and fitting or trying dentures in the mouth. However, it is not illegal for dental technicians to work directly to the public. Nor is it illegal for technicians to advertise their services as long as they do not hold themselves out that they practise dentistry, or are prepared to practise dentistry.

Dentists, dental hygienists and dental therapists are currently registered with the Council, and plans are progressing to enable the GDC to register dental technicians in the future. When this is introduced all registrants will be individually accountable to the Council, with dentists additionally accountable as leaders of the team.'

H – Signing forms

Danesh is a new associate in another practice in town who has qualified and completed his VT year in a different region. You meet at a British Dental Association (BDA) function and ask him how he is getting on. He says that he is enjoying working in the practice which seems to be very successful, although he does seem to be signing a lot of forms that the practice manager (who is also the wife of the practice principal) presents to him each week. He does not always have time to read these before signing them, as she stands over him and appears impatient if he delays.

Background information

You are the principal of the only other practice in town. As far as you can tell, both practices have about the same number of NHS and private patients, but the other practice always seems to be able to afford new equipment and have longer holidays than your practice. Danesh tells you that he has queried the number of forms that he is signing and the practice manager has explained that, as he is an associate, he can sign forms for the principal of the practice to claim for work that has been undertaken.

What should you do, and what should you say to Danesh?

It would be advisable for you, as a practice principal yourself, to suggest to Danesh that he should consult his defence organisation. He should be, or should quickly make himself, aware of the regulations relating to signing forms for treatment that has been carried out by another practitioner. All dental graduates should consider why their signature has value and credibility, and what they need to do to protect its use.

I – The rules apply to someone else

Kitty is your new VDP. She seems to have plenty of self-confidence and enjoys the challenge of general dental practice. Although you have explained practice policy regarding the referral of orthodontic patients (they are all referred to the local specialist practice), one of your nurses tells you that Kitty is fitting removable appliances without reference to the specialist practice.

Background information

During Kitty's elective time as a student she worked in a hospital orthodontic clinic with an NHS consultant, seeing new patients and fitting and adjusting removable appliances. The consultant was not complimentary about specialist orthodontic practitioners, and so she feels that she should diagnose and treat simple malocclusions. She says that if she cannot manage the case she will refer it to the consultant.

What should you do?

From the information given above there is no evidence that Kitty has caused any problems with her management of orthodontic cases so far. However, problems could arise in the future – she may get it wrong and cause a problem; and, of course, what happens to her patients who are under treatment when her vocational training year comes to an end? There will clearly be sound reasons why your practice has adopted this policy regarding orthodontic referrals, and you need to meet with Kitty and explain again that she is exceeding her authority in behaving in the way that she is. This should be backed up with a written warning. It would also be prudent to try to persuade her to reassess her views on specialist practitioners: Kitty may find herself in another part of the country where they may be the only source of orthodontic treatment available within a reasonable timeframe and travelling distance.

ETHICS AND LAW FOR THE DENTAL TEAM

J – How can I work under these conditions?

Rhodri is a new VDP in your practice. He is asking for a particular make of composite restorative material that is much more expensive than the one that you have in use for everyone in the practice (and of which you have at least two unopened boxes in the store cupboard).

Background information

You have no reason to suspect that the composite that you are currently using is in any way inferior to the make your VDP wants to use. Rhodri says that his teachers at the dental school told him that the material he wants to use is the best on the market and that general dental practitioners always want to use the cheapest option. He has been telling his patients that he cannot do a decent job for them as you have refused to supply him with proper quality materials.

What should you do?

Rhodri needs to learn fast that just because materials used in the practice are different from those he has used in the dental hospital, this does not necessarily make them inferior. A common complaint by vocational trainers is that even new dental graduates can have fixed ideas about what is acceptable, in terms of both treatments and materials. Some further discussion between Rhodri and his trainer is called for, in order to reach a compromise or resolution. Of course, there might be situations where a VDP is justified in protesting about poor-quality materials or equipment. In such cases, he or she should discuss this first with his or her trainer, and then with the vocational training adviser or regional adviser for vocational training.

Training practices are expected to meet high standards, and can be removed from the list of training practices, thus having the training contract cancelled – even during a training year in extreme cases. Most trainers work extremely hard to create an effective training environment in their practice and to develop an excellent rapport with their VDP. However, postgraduate deans and VT advisors take VDP complaints seriously when the trainer is not meeting his or her commitments. Support and advice will often do the trick, but the more draconian sanctions are there to be used as and when appropriate.

K – Who is responsible?

Richard has been working as a hygienist in the practice for over a year and he has been asked to carry out subgingival root debridement on a patient who is undergoing a prolonged course of chemotherapy and has a Hickman line in place. The referring dentist, who is just about to retire, has referred the patient and has given a verbal opinion that antibiotic cover is not required. Richard approaches you as the other principal in the practice as he is not sure what to do and the patient is unhappy about the possibility of his treatment being cancelled.

Background information

The referring practitioner refers infrequently to the hygienist and does not see the value of your wish to develop the dental team. You are already aware that he is not keeping his continuing professional development (CPD) up to date as he feels it is unnecessary as he is going to retire within the next two years.

What should you do?

A number of issues need to be resolved in this case. It is important that members of the practice team not only understand the need to balance appropriate referral, treatment planning and prescription with personal professional responsibility and personal accountability for acts and omissions, but also how vicarious liability can affect the team. You should base your advice to Richard on the latest antibiotic prescribing guidelines, and recommend that he refuses to treat the patient unless or until advice from the patient's general practitioner or oncologist has verified in writing whether there is or is not a need for cover. There is a danger that the dentist involved in the referral could claim, if there was a subsequent problem, that he had no responsibility for the hygienist undertaking the treatment without antibiotic cover as dental professionals are expected to take responsibility for their own actions.

Richard should be able to talk with the referring practitioner to discuss the issues. It may be helpful to refer Richard to the advice in the *British National Formulary* (*BNF*) or any useful recent articles on the need for antibiotic cover such as the British Antimicrobial Society Guidelines (see Chapter 10), and also to advise him to contact his defence organisation for additional support and advice. If Richard is unwilling to approach your colleague alone it may be helpful for you to accompany him.

Subsequently, it would be appropriate to arrange a staff development meeting to discuss the practice approach to the use of antibiotic cover and to ensure that all staff in the dental team clearly understand each other's roles and individual responsibility to maintain competence, put patient's interests first and co-operate with other members in the team in the best interest of the patients.

L – Negligence

Your patient, Mr Eschion, is a middle-aged professional gentleman and is attending your practice for the first time. He has previously been a regular attender with Mr Mye O'Pyia, who has recently retired. Your clinical examination reveals bleeding on probing in all sextants, generalised increased pocket depth, and some mobility of teeth. Radiographs reveal generalised horizontal bone loss of 3–4 mm together with some infra-bony pockets, and two teeth that are so badly affected that they require extraction. You explain the clinical situation to Mr Eschion, who says 'Is that what you meant by "Another Mye O'Pyia mess"?' You had muttered these words under your breath (so you thought) when you saw the radiographs. He is one of several patients from that practice who have extensive untreated periodontal problems. You know that Mr Mye O'Pyia did not employ a hygienist. He believed that his patients did not need a 'wee girl' to show them how to brush their teeth. Mr Eschion tells you that he wants you to write a letter to his solicitors detailing the negligence of his former dentist.

What should you do?

You are entitled to your professional opinion, but it is not your responsibility to determine if your former colleague has been negligent – that is a matter for a court. You should not respond to Mr Eschion's request by writing a letter to his solicitors claiming negligence, no matter how strongly you feel on the subject. You should point out to Mr Eschion that you are unaware of the circumstances of his previous treatment, and cannot comment on the treatment that he did or did not receive. However, you are able to say that it is improbable that the current periodontal situation has arisen suddenly.

A few weeks later you receive a letter from Mr Eschion's solicitors.

Dear Sir,

Our Client: Mr Rhys Eschion, Dunchewin, Flossingham

Our client has instructed us to seek a report from you regarding his general oral and gum condition as he is seeking damages in relation to treatment that he has received from his previous general dental practitioner.

Please find attached a signed declaration from our client authorising the release of his dental records and requesting the submission of this report to our office.

We will pay your reasonable fees for the compilation and submission of this report.

Our client informs us that you have other patients who have recently attended your practice from the same source, and with similar problems. We would be grateful if you could provide us with their names and addresses so that we may offer our services.

Yours faithfully,

Mr I Soodem

What should you do?

Having received a formal letter from your patient's solicitors you are now able to submit your report. You should seek the help of your indemnity agency in drafting your report. The report should be a factual account of the situation as it was presented to you. If you offer an opinion within the report, you must be prepared to defend this in a court of law.

The solicitor is being very unprofessional in the last paragraph of his letter and is encouraging you to be unprofessional also. You should not release the names or addresses of any of your patients without their consent.

M – Orthodontic retainer

You are an orthodontic specialist registrar who is 'on call' for the management of orthodontic problems. Jemima is a 20-year-old student who has been sent to the hospital by a local specialist practice because her fixed orthodontic retainer has become detached.

Background information

Jemima underwent a course of fixed appliance orthodontics under private contract with a local specialist practitioner, which was completed six months previously. The appliances were removed and the retainer placed by a general dental practitioner who attended the specialist practice for one session per week to gain orthodontic experience. When the bonded retainer became detached she returned to the specialist practice which told her that, as she had been discharged, she would have to pay a fee of £75.00 to have a new retainer made and placed. She complained that the contract included placement of a retainer, although the period of retention was unspecified. The practice was adamant that they had fulfilled their contract and that unless she was prepared to pay she should go to the local hospital orthodontic unit for the replacement.

What should you do?

This is a very difficult situation. You are being asked to commit hospital resources to manage a problem that has arisen subsequent to treatment provided in the primary care sector under private contract. Your hospital may have a policy that will address this problem – if so, it should be followed. If not, you are faced with the dilemma of a patient who may, or may not, require further retention and who has been told that you will sort out her problem. Without seeing the initial malocclusion and treatment details you cannot tell if further retention is required.

If this was a case where a practitioner had attempted an extraction, encountered difficulties and referred the patient as an emergency there would be no real dilemma as the patient has clearly got a condition that will directly affect their health. The missing retainer is not an immediate or direct threat to health, in spite of what the patient might think. A good ethical practice will already have a complaints mechanism in place and Jemima could seek redress through that route.

The GDC have produced a guidance document 'Principles of Complaints Handling' and practices should follow the advice given. In April 2004, the Healthcare Commission took over responsibility for regulating and inspecting the independent healthcare sector in England. They may be able to offer help if the practitioner is registered with the Healthcare Commission. They are unable to help with the return of fees or other monies paid, and orthodontists are not obliged to register with the Commission unless they provide dental treatment under general anaesthesia (www.healthcarecommission.org.uk/Homepage/fs/en).

Jemima may also be able to get help via the Sale of Goods Act 1979, amended in 2002 by the Sale and Supply of Goods to Consumers Regulations. If an item has a fault that is present at the time of sale (which may be a 'latent' or 'inherent' fault), the consumer can complain once it is discovered. Buyers cannot, however, expect a legal remedy in respect of:

- fair wear and tear
- misuse or accidental damage.

She will need to demonstrate that the retainer was faulty at the time of placement. As the retainer was placed by a non-specialist, this may assist her case.

In dealing with all of these scenarios, there is an element of 'Well, it depends ...'. We have suggested what we believe to be sensible, well-founded advice in each case; we do not believe that these are the only responses that would be appropriate. Much of being a professional is about developing the professional wisdom and judgement to be able to deal with such situations – especially if that means knowing when to ask for help and advice. The next chapter examines in greater depth the nature of professionalism in practice.

CHAPTER 8
PROFESSIONALISM IN PRACTICE

CHAPTER 8
PROFESSIONALISM IN PRACTICE

Dental professionals are expected to behave in a professional manner. Recently in the UK, some high-profile medico-legal cases have brought the issue of professional behaviour of clinicians into sharp focus. Sir Donald Irvine, a past president of the General Medical Council, has said that the medical profession is at a crossroads, the choice being to persevere with the traditional, paternalistic doctor-centred approach or to move to a patient-centred approach to care.[1] Dentistry and the dental team face similar issues.[2]

Dentistry – a profession or a business?

Before attempting to define professional behaviour in a dental professional, it is necessary to distinguish between dentistry as a profession and as a business, and decide whether such a distinction matters.

One of the elements of professionalism is altruism,[3] (see below). Although economic factors should not take precedence, the dentist, as the leader of a team of healthcare workers, has a duty to behave with financial responsibility towards his or her staff, as well as providing for his or her own family. A balance must be found between the ethical behaviour expected of a health professional and that of a business person. Welie[4] defines a profession as:

> 'a collective of expert service providers who have jointly and publicly committed to always give priority to the existential needs and interests of the public they serve above their own and who in turn are trusted by the public to do so.'

'Existential need' is relief of pain or threat to health. This implies that dentistry is only a profession because the public recognises that title through the provision of treatment that leads to health gain or prevention of health loss. Should the behaviour of dental professionals move in a different direction, or at a speed different from that expected by the public, dentists may lose their professional status, and hence their right to self-regulation. Welie[5] argues that not all treatment provided by the dentist contributes directly to the oral health of the patient and hence, by definition, is not a professional activity. This does not, however, imply that the dentist is 'incompetent, dishonest or otherwise immoral ...', or absolve the dentist from acting in an appropriate manner. It simply means that procedures that may be carried out by the dentist, such as tooth whitening, have currently no proved health benefits, even though social mores may lead to considerable demand of the dentist as the natural provider. It further suggests that an increasing emphasis on cosmetic dentistry may make it difficult, ultimately, to distinguish between the type of service provided by the dentist and that of, say, the hairdresser.

Dentists and doctors are trusted by the majority of the population, whereas 60% of the public do not trust business people to tell the truth.[6] The public are particularly concerned about responsibility, integrity and honesty in the business world. The Institute of Business Ethics also discriminates between business ethics (how a company conducts itself while making a profit), and an ethical business (making a positive contribution to the community). The Institute seeks to encourage high standards of behaviour in the business world and research has shown that companies that have a code of ethics outperformed similar companies that had no such code.

Although the primary aim of business is to make a profit and that of dentistry is to provide appropriate healthcare, the behaviour of the dentist in practice can easily conform to the code of business ethics. The dental practice must make sufficient money to reward all staff adequately and provide sufficient surplus to invest in practice improvements such as refurbishment or staff development.

Attributes of professional behaviour

The Institute for International Medical Education has listed the attributes of professional behaviour as: altruism, accountability, duty, excellence, honour and integrity, and respect for others.[3] This is an extension of the Georgetown Mantra (see Chapter 5). An explanation of these terms, with some examples, follows. It is important to realise that these concepts, and their relationship to contemporary medical and dental care, are continually under scrutiny and review. Those who wish to keep up to date with the debate should consult the Picker Institute website (see Chapter 10).

Altruism

Meaning: Placing other people – especially patients – before self.

Example: It is a quarter to five on a Friday afternoon. You are a general dental practitioner; you and your dental nurse are the only people left in the practice. You have a windsurfing weekend planned with friends. It is a two-hour journey away and you had agreed to meet there at seven o'clock. Just as you are about to leave, a mother arrives with her child who has fallen over and fractured an incisor. Both mother and child are upset. It is clear that the fracture has exposed the pulp.

The altruistic dentist will stay and provide the necessary treatment to render the child pain-free, even though it means they will be late meeting their friends.

Accountability

Meaning: You are answerable for what you do, or do not do. You may be answerable to your patient, your team, your employer, your professional body, or to society. You may be accountable for your own work, or for that of others.

Example: A patient attends with a carious mandibular third permanent molar tooth. You decide that the tooth must be extracted and proceed to do so. During the extraction a root fractures, and a difficult surgical removal of the root leaves the patient with paraesthesia of the lip.

You must be prepared to defend your decision to remove the tooth (answerable for what you do) and why you did not discuss the possibility of nerve damage with the patient beforehand, or offer alternative treatments for the tooth (answerable for what you did not do).

Duty

Meaning: Accepting that you have a responsibility to provide care (sometimes called 'duty of care'; a lack of duty of care is NEGLIGENCE), to work for the welfare of the profession and community. Duty of care relates to beneficence (doing good) and non-maleficence (doing no harm).

Example:

- **Duty of care** – A patient attends your practice with a severe malocclusion. You can see that there are both dental health and aesthetic benefits to be gained by treatment. However, you do not have the skills to provide this treatment competently. Your duty of care says that you should refer the patient to a competent provider, such as an orthodontic consultant or specialist orthodontic practitioner. The principle of non-maleficence operates here – you would be doing harm by trying to provide such treatment yourself.

- **Welfare of the profession** – If you have particular knowledge or skills that would benefit the profession, eg you have good writing and organisational skills, you might serve the profession by becoming the editor of a journal, or, if you have a natural grasp of complex situations together with an ability to explain complex issues in a straightforward manner, then you might consider standing for election to a body such as the British Dental Association or the General Dental Council.

- **Welfare of the community** – As a dentist or dental professional you may be asked your views on water fluoridation. It is your duty to the community to advocate the adjustment of the concentration of fluoride in the water to optimal levels to provide maximum benefit to the community. One of the high profile medico-legal cases referred to earlier in this chapter was that of Harold Shipman, a general medical practitioner who murdered his patients. Any GP or hospital consultant in charge of the care of one of Shipman's patients had a duty to report his concerns about Shipman's care of the patient to a relevant authority such as the NHS primary care trust (at that time, the local family health services authority or FHSA) responsible for Dr Shipman. Such reporting is known as 'whistle-blowing'. This case also embraces the welfare of the profession.

Excellence

Meaning: Striving to continuously improve your knowledge and skills. This will include a commitment to lifelong learning.

Example: When you have been in practice for some time, you will notice that new materials and/or techniques become available that you are unfamiliar with. If these are proved to be an improvement over the materials or techniques that you use, then you should ensure that you attend an appropriate course that will bring you up to date, so that your patients may benefit from your improved skills and the use of new materials. This is an example of evidence-based practice.

Honour and integrity

Meaning: Being honest, truthful, keeping confidences and doing what you say you will. In addition, it means not misusing your professional status.

Example: A middle-aged patient attends your practice for the first time. Your examination shows that there are several missing teeth, as well as restorative and periodontal needs. In compiling your treatment plan you discuss with the patient the replacement of the missing teeth by means of a denture. You must draw the patient's attention to the fact that a tissue-borne denture would not be in their best long-term dental health interests, and that a tooth-borne denture would be better, although you do not provide the latter under the NHS.

Respect for others

Meaning: Behaving to others in a way that you would like them to behave towards yourself. This includes your relationships with patients, their parents or carers, members of your immediate team, students, and other dentists and doctors. This philosophy has been called 'humanism'. More recently, the concept of 'emotional intelligence' has been proposed, which expands on humanism by looking at two aspects of intelligence: understanding yourself, your goals, intentions, responses and behaviour; and understanding others and their feelings.

Example: You are a member of staff supervising students who are just starting to treat patients in the clinic. One student tries to deliver an inferior dental nerve block using a needle that is usually used for infiltration. Respect for the student may be shown by taking the student away from the chairside to discuss their reasons for choosing that needle, and then giving your reasons why it is inappropriate for the proposed procedure. Humiliation of the student in front of the patient and dental nurse, either by a 'telling off' or by sarcasm, is disrespectful and unprofessional.

Professional behaviour and clinical governance

A recent definition of professional behaviour[4] has been given above; the Oxford English Dictionary provides a broader definition of a profession:

'An occupation whose core element is work based upon the mastery of a complex body of knowledge and skills. It is a vocation in which knowledge of some department of science or learning or the practice of an art founded upon it is used in the service of others. Its members profess a commitment to competence, integrity and morality, altruism, and the promotion of the public good within their domain. These commitments form the basis of a social contract between a profession and society, which in return grants the profession the right to autonomy in practice and the privilege of self-regulation. Professions and their members are accountable to those serviced and to society.'

Clinical governance was introduced to the NHS by the government in 1998. It is defined as:[7]

'A framework through which NHS organisations are accountable for continually improving the quality of their services and safeguarding high standards of care by creating an environment in which excellence in clinical care will flourish.'

Careful inspection of this definition will show that all the points made for clinical governance are included in the attributes of a professional. The justification for clinical governance arises from perceived shortcomings in the delivery of care – partly as a result of failures by the professions to regulate themselves adequately, and partly due to a concern that government policy has made quality subservient to quantity and cost of care.

Clinical governance provides a framework within which many aspects of quality care may be co-ordinated and managed and is generally applied to organisations, whereas professional behaviour works at an individual and internal level. Individuals, of course, must actively contribute to clinical governance, and indeed this is part of the duty of a professional. Furthermore, the mechanisms of clinical governance are able to identify the poorly performing practitioner, and to provide remedial support for that individual, which, in turn, will raise the overall quality of care delivered by the organisation. Failure to respond to remediation by the poorly performing individual will lead to disciplinary action for the protection of patients. All NHS organisations have an individual who is responsible for the management of clinical governance.

Since its introduction the principles of clinical governance have been adapted and modified by various organisations. The original tenets of clinical governance are:

- consultation and patient involvement
- clinical risk management
- clinical audit
- research and effectiveness
- staffing and staff management
- education, training and continuing personal and professional development
- evidence-based practice.

These basic tenets remain, although they may have different titles within different organisations. Clinical governance should be seen as another means by which professional behaviour and ethical conduct may be promoted and monitored, particularly in relation to the quality of care.

CHAPTER 9
AUDIT, RESEARCH AND EVIDENCE-BASED PRACTICE

CHAPTER 9
AUDIT, RESEARCH AND EVIDENCE-BASED PRACTICE

The contemporary undergraduate dental course encourages students to become involved with both audit and research activity, and to practise evidence-based dentistry. Certain dental professional courses also require some form of research or audit activity, and an understanding of evidence-based dental practice. This chapter gives an overview of the differences between research and audit, focusing, in particular, on the ethical considerations. It also provides information regarding evidence-based practice, and how it fits in with audit and research.

Clinical audit

Clinical audit has been defined as seeking to 'improve patient care and outcomes through the systematic review of care against explicit criteria and the implementation of change'[1] and it forms part of the structure of clinical governance (see Chapter 8). It has been argued that 'audit' is an inappropriate word for the activity carried out under its umbrella. Terms that might be more descriptive (and less likely to be associated with the financial connotations of the word) are 'dental care evaluation', 'clinical and administrative review', 'self-scrutiny' and 'quality assurance'.[2] Audit activity may be arbitrarily divided in a variety of ways, eg:

- internal or external
- clinical or non-clinical
- structure, process or outcome.

Internal audit takes place within a practice, where the clinician may explore an aspect of care provided, such as the quality of dental panoramic radiographs. **External audit** takes place on a larger scale, where a large number of practices are invited to submit dental panoramic radiographs to a central body as part of a regional or national audit, for example. These are examples of **clinical audit**.

Non-clinical audit might involve a hospital department exploring the number and source of referrals. Examples of audit of structure, process or outcome are:

- Structure – Is there appropriate resource (such as dental chairs) to provide treatment for our practice patients?
- Process – How long patients wait before they receive treatment.
- Outcome – see example below.

Typically, audit is described as a cycle (Figure 9.1).

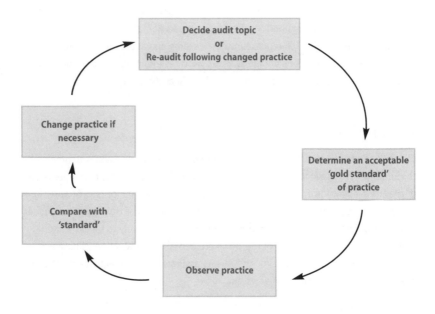

Figure 9.1 Audit cycle.

An individual or group of individuals chooses a topic on which they wish to undertake an outcome audit (eg the longevity of composite build-ups on fractured maxillary incisor teeth). The group will then determine their own gold standard of practice, which might be that 100% of composite build-ups should not normally need replacing within five years. This is then observed. Practically speaking, using this example, they will need to use retrospective data, ie go back through their files or computer records and pull out all the patients who have received such treatment five or more years ago. Shorter-term audits can be prospective, eg waiting for the occurrence of an event such as the accidental loss of an orthodontic bracket over a three-month period.

Having obtained this information, they will compare their individual success rate with that of the 'gold standard'. If they meet that standard the audit is recorded as successfully completed. If they do not meet that standard, then they need to explore the possible reasons why:

- Their 'gold standard' is unreasonable, despite the earlier discussions when setting the standard. In this case the standard should be altered.

- Some individuals within the group are achieving the standard, whereas others are not.

In the latter case the differences may arise for a variety of reasons, such as:

- use of different materials

- use of different technique

- differences in the severity of the original condition.

The differences in clinical procedure between the 'successful' and 'unsuccessful' practitioners may then be explored and in the 'unsuccessful' cases clinical practice altered. After an interval the audit should be repeated to see if the altered practice is more successful. Thus audit becomes a repeated circuit rather than a simple circle. Audit may prompt practitioners to maintain or improve their clinical skills by taking part in a relevant continuing professional education course.

From the example above it is easy to see how audit may improve the quality of patient care. It has the advantage of being led and delivered by clinicians and is therefore 'owned' by those who are using it. Some will find this scrutiny of practice invasive and threatening and it is important that the activity is carried out in a supportive manner.

There are disadvantages to audit.[3] The results of audit can lead to a change of practice, which is its main *raison d'être*. However, this change can be implemented immediately, regardless of the quality of the project, the quality (or lack) of statistical analysis, and without any form of peer review other than by those who carried out the project. Acting on the results of a poorly designed project can be dangerous and is certainly unethical. It is therefore important that those undertaking and leading audit are experienced in such activity, are aware of the pitfalls that may lie in their path and act in an ethical and professional manner when conducting the audit. It is beyond the scope of this textbook to provide more extensive information regarding audit, but there are many textbooks, journals and websites which can provide the interested reader with further information on clinical audit.

Research

The Economic and Social Research Council (ESRC) defines research as: 'any form of disciplined enquiry that aims to contribute to a body of knowledge or theory.'[4] Table 9.1 lists differences between research and audit.

Table 9.1. Differences between research and audit. Adapted from The Royal College of Psychiatrists[5]

Research	Audit
Aims to establish what is best practice	Aims to evaluate how close practice is to best practice and to identify ways of improving the quality of healthcare provided
Is designed so that it can be replicated and that its results can be generalised to other similar groups	Is specific and local to one particular patient group – results are not transferable to other settings
Aims to generate new knowledge/increase the sum of knowledge	Aims to improve services
Is usually initiated by researchers and university-led	Is usually led by service providers and takes place in primary and secondary care sectors

Research	Audit
Is theory-driven/usually involves testing a hypothesis	Is practice-based Compares observed practice with an agreed 'gold standard'
Is often supported financially by a grant. The scientific aspects of the paper (including statistical analysis) will have been scrutinised and approved by the grant-awarding body	Virtually no support unless a regional or national project and therefore no prior scrutiny of scientific quality or of proposed statistical analysis
Usually requires prior approval from an ethics committee	Usually no prior scrutiny of proposed survey
Is often a one-off study	Is an ongoing process
May involve allocating service users randomly to different treatment groups	Never involves allocating patients randomly to different treatment groups
May involve administration of a placebo	Never involves a placebo treatment
May involve a completely new treatment	Never involves a completely new treatment
The observer may be unaware of the particular treatment provided (blind)	The observer knows what treatment has been provided
The outcome of the study will usually be submitted for publication in a peer-reviewed journal	The outcome may occasionally be published, usually only if it is a large-scale (regional or national) audit project
Researchers will gain status and reward on the basis of research conducted	Usually no reward for audit project unless it has significant impact

Ethics of research

Whenever research that involves hypothesis testing on human beings is undertaken, the researchers must protect the rights of the individuals who are invited to take part in the project. This involves the researchers obtaining **consent**. This is similar to that described earlier in Chapters 5 and 6. The subjects must give informed, written consent, they must have the capacity and competence to give consent, and consent should be obtained without duress or inducement. They should have the freedom to withdraw from the project at any time without prejudice and have the expectation that their individual records will remain confidential at all times. The researchers have an obligation to minimise risk to the subjects.

The ethics of medical (and dental) research are driven by the World Medical Association Declaration of Helsinki – Ethical principles for medical investigation on human beings. The Declaration was first adopted in 1964 and has since undergone several revisions to accommodate advances in medical science and ethical problems.[6] It provides guidance on medical research ethics involving research on people, identifiable human material or identifiable data, and includes principles on:

- safeguarding research subjects
- informed consent
- minimising risk
- adhering to an approved research plan/protocol.

Anyone planning a research project will need to obtain agreement from a research ethics committee (sometimes called a 'human investigation committee') whose role is to scrutinise the project protocol and to ensure that participants in the project will be protected and that the study conforms to the Declaration of Helsinki guidelines. There may, in addition, be a scientific scrutiny committee, whose role is to ensure that the structure of the project is scientifically sound. This will include looking at sample size – it is unethical to conduct a research project with too few subjects to show or not show a difference (and it is also unethical to include too many subjects, which would waste time and resources) – and the proposed use of statistical analysis of the data to ensure that it is appropriate. These processes, while time-consuming and occasionally frustrating, are there not only to protect the subject, but also to protect the researcher.

The research ethics committee will be particularly interested in the information that is provided to the potential subjects. This must be written, using language that the subject can understand, and supported by a verbal explanation from an individual who is involved with the project. It is good practice to have two consent forms, one for the subject to keep and one to be kept on file with the researcher. The consent forms must be signed and dated by the subject and by the researcher. Occasionally it is prudent to have a witness present who can also sign the consent form. A comprehensive consent form should include information on:

- research aims
- research methods
- sources of funding
- possible conflicts of interest
- institutional affiliations of the researchers
- anticipated benefits of the study
- publication and dissemination of results
- potential risks of the study (this should include potential risks to the fetus for women who are pregnant or who might become pregnant during the research programme)
- any discomfort that might be entailed
- potential impact on eligibility for life insurance or private medical insurance as a result of the study (including information that might be obtained as part of the study, such as identification of a genetic predisposition to a given medical condition)
- the right to abstain from participation
- the right to withdraw consent to participate at any time
- complaint-handling procedures
- the use of placebos; if placebos will be given to some subjects, what chance each subject has of getting the study drug/treatment
- the drug or device under test and the stage of development (a short description)
- the dosage of the drug and method of administration where drugs are administered.

Funding body

Very little research carried out is not supported by funding from an external body. This may be government funding (eg via the ESRC or the Medical Research Council (MRC)), through charities such as Cancer Research UK, or through a pharmaceutical company (see below). These bodies have a responsibility to ensure that projects they fund are scientifically sound. They will look carefully at the project protocol. A project which is scientifically unsound is automatically unethical. A scientifically sound project can still be unethical, however, and many research bodies ask for research ethics approval from a local committee (or committees if it is a multi-centre project) to accompany the grant application.

Consent for children or those who do not have capacity

This is a challenging area for researchers. Inevitably children get ill, and new treatments must be tested to gauge their efficacy against established treatment regimens. Similarly, those whose condition renders them unable to give informed consent may benefit from a new treatment. Under these circumstances it is the parent or carer who must give consent.

The general advice regarding research involving children or those with special needs is to try to find alternative means of conducting the study wherever possible. The aims should always be to protect potentially vulnerable members of society and to uphold public trust in the profession. Although parental consent is mandatory, it is good practice to ensure the child receives the information regarding the project and gives their consent. If a child becomes upset during a procedure, that must be considered to represent withdrawal of their consent. For those undertaking social research (eg by questionnaire) the Market Research Society (MRS) website and the British Sociological Association have appropriate guidelines.[7,8] The MRC provides further advice on the ethics of clinical and/or therapeutic research in children.[9]

Research using the Internet

An emerging phenomenon is the use of the Internet for research. The Association of Internet Research has produced guidelines for those who wish to use the Internet for such purposes.[10] Particular challenges facing researchers who wish to recruit via the Internet are essentially those of verification, consent and confidentiality. Without face-to-face interaction the researcher cannot be sure that the person they are contacting is who they say they are, and this has knock-on effects when trying to obtain consent. Finally, unless there are secure links established – preferably password-protected – any information sent to the researcher via the Internet should not be considered confidential.

The Hinxton Group consensus statement

The Hinxton Group is an international consortium of ethicists and researchers on stem cells who met in Hinxton, Cambridgeshire, UK in February 2006.[11] The group is concerned about the ethics and law of its research area. Stem cell research is at the 'cutting edge' of research and is controversial. It frequently involves international teams working together. Some countries have an absolute ban on such research, and their researchers are unable to participate in any way – even if the stem cells are physically in a different country. Although frustrating, this is at least straightforward. Other countries have vague guidelines which leave potential researchers in doubt over their position. The statement is designed to bring clarity and order to a confused situation for researchers and for editors of journals who may be asked to publish the findings of such research.

Pharmaceutical trials and healthy volunteers

As the majority of research is university-led, many drug trials are carried out by university staff, and they will often recruit volunteers from the student body. There may be an incentive to take part as the volunteers can be paid for their time and trouble, which is helpful when managing student debt. It is important that the money offered does not become an inducement, and that staff do not put undue pressure on students to participate. It is also important that students behave in a responsible manner. The use of the drug on healthy adults suggests that the company is looking for side-effects of a new product. A case of a student who enrolled on two separate drug trials, without disclosing their participation to either party, unfortunately ended tragically when there was an interaction between the drugs and the student died.

More recently in the UK, a trial of a new monoclonal antibody called TGN1412 using eight healthy volunteers caused an unprecedented, unexpected and almost fatal reaction in six of the volunteers (the remaining two were given a placebo), a reaction that had not occurred in tests on animals. This has prompted a review of the process of testing new drugs, particularly drugs of this type.

Scientific fraud

Even if the research that was carried out was ethical, there may still be problems with the reporting of the project. It is not unknown for researchers to fabricate data. If the research has been sponsored by an industrial company, who have analysed the data, they may 'cherry pick' results that are supportive of their product and ignore findings that would be unhelpful. Journals who publish scientific work are naturally concerned about the ill repute that fraud brings, both to the scientific community and to their journal in particular.[12] Other examples of dubious practice include inappropriate authorship (eg a head of department whose policy is that his or her name appears on all publications from their department regardless of their involvement); not reporting data that contradict your own prior research; bowing to pressure from the sponsoring organisation to change the design, methodology or results; and, most prevalent of all, not keeping adequate records.[13]

Honesty is essential in these matters, despite the commercial pressures involved in the development of a new drug or the academic pressures of being 'research active' for return in the UK's Research Assessment Exercise (which allocates substantial government funding to universities on the basis of the amount of grant money attracted and number and quality of publications).

Evidence-based practice

Is it ethical to practise dentistry that is not evidence based?

'Evidence-based medicine is the conscientious, explicit and judicious use of current best evidence in making decisions about the care of individual patients.' (David Sackett, 1996)[14]

In the past, dentistry has had a preoccupation with output and there appeared to be little awareness of the need to control the introduction of treatments which were not effective or unproved. There was a tendency to continue with an ineffective intervention if there was no better option to replace it. The document, *A First Class Service – Quality in the NHS* (1998) (see Chapter 8) described clinical governance as 'a system for improving the quality of clinical practice' and clearly the use of evidence-based healthcare is part of this.

Nowadays we accept that the way we choose and provide treatment for our patients must be based on evidence that shows that what we have decided to do has been tried and tested to show it is safe. We must ask ourselves whether we are able to complete the treatment successfully provided we have assessed the situation correctly. As outlined in the *Standards for Dental Professionals* from the GDC, the team should not put their patients at risk and must act in the best interest of their patients. We should never undertake any treatment or use any technique unless we are satisfied it will achieve the outcome we are seeking and has been agreed with our patients. Providing healthcare that is only based on evidence involves assessing the effectiveness, efficiency and the appropriateness of the care offered. A simpler way of looking at it is to ensure that we care for our patients by providing the right treatment for the right patient in the right way, at the right time, in the right place, at the right cost!

The clinical effectiveness of a procedure is a balance between the patient's and professionals' view of the condition and the intervention. We have a responsibility not to undertake a treatment if the evidence shows that it would do more harm than good or if it is of unknown effect, but we may feel confident if the procedure we are considering is of unknown effect but in a good-quality research programme. Ensuring this means we need to look at the information available and at research from reputable sources.

Our day-to-day decisions for our patients are influenced by a range of factors, particularly as new information is always becoming available and we know our knowledge and memory deteriorate with time. Often our choice of treatment or material is influenced by the resources available to us, the fear of litigation, the experience of the last patient outcome and the payment system involved. The results of audit, our experience of continuing education and training, and the evidence we can find are often considered less important as they are also time-consuming and require a real commitment. The team members all need to keep as up to date as possible by reading, discussing with colleagues and attending courses and even arranging team audits and journal clubs.

But how do we find the evidence?

The team needs to spend time developing the ability to find information and then interpret and evaluate it (in this case 'the team' might be members of the practice, or it may be a study group or journal club that involves members of several different practices). The four basic routes are to:

- ask an expert (who could be wrong)
- read a textbook (usually out of date)
- find an article (as long as it is not biased)
- search a database (not reviewed).

In order to comply with evidence-based practice we need to:

- identify the problem
- search for evidence
- make sense of the evidence
- discard poor research and act on good evidence
- store and update the evidence.

From the above it is clear why an understanding of research is considered an important element of an undergraduate dental course. Evidence-based practice aims to provide the best possible evidence at the point of clinical contact. We need to ask questions about the care we want to provide, ie is it actually going to be effective? We then need to ask ourselves what evidence would provide an answer, what studies, journals or books might help, what information sources would be most reliable. A good team will be able to ask the right questions, know where to look for evidence, and then be able to assess the quality of that evidence.

The Centre for Evidence-based Dentistry has outlined a method for critical appraisal and it guides us to ask a number of questions to start with:

- Can you trust the results?
- What are the results telling us and how relevant or useful are they?
- Are the results clinically important?

A problem-solving approach is often a good place to start – discussing within the team what works and seeking out the best available evidence from books, journals and possibly the Internet. Critical appraisal of both the strength and quality of the evidence is essential as the technique helps us to make sense of the evidence, assess the reliability and relevance of the information and guide us to accurate interpretation.

Some of the evidence has already been identified and appraised in systematic reviews already undertaken on the available evidence. The Cochrane Collaboration prepares, maintains and disseminates systematic reviews of the effects of healthcare. In a systematic review, authors systematically review the evidence and grade it with respect to its value. Potential benefit to health ranges from beneficial to unknown to could be effective or harmful.

Clinical guidelines are also available. Guidelines used in conjunction with clinical experience provide guidance on what to do in a given clinical situation. Guidelines are usually produced by an authoritative body such as a specialist society or a Royal College. Departure from published guidelines in clinical practice may have unpleasant consequences for the practitioner if treatment does not proceed smoothly.

Finally, we need to decide how we will manage difficult situations when perhaps the evidence is not clear or we can find little information to support our choices. For most of the procedures that are carried out in dentistry there is no sound and reliable evidence, and we rely on 'custom and practice' as a way forward, practising in a reasonable manner, ie doing what most professionals would do in similar circumstances. What if a dental professional is referred a patient and the treatment plan is not based on evidence? Should the dental professional carry on or challenge the decision? Problems also may arise when companies develop a new technique or material, for example, and the only research available is that carried out by the company promoting the product. In dentistry we may try a technique but we soon discard it if we do not achieve success for our patients. The dilemma is, do we believe that is an ethical way to behave?

> **An example of an unethical study that has provided a lasting evidence base for dental practice – evidence for the aetiology of caries**
>
> A famous study conducted into the aetiology of caries was carried out in Vipeholm from 1945 to 1953.[15] Vipeholm Hospital was an institute for those with special needs near Malmö in southern Sweden. The inmates were given refined carbohydrates (sweets and/or sticky toffee), either associated with mealtimes, or spread throughout the day. No consent was sought for this study. The results of this study provided sound evidence to support the implication of the timing and type of sugar ingestion in the aetiology of dental caries. A recent paper defended the ethical issues that have subsequently been raised regarding this study. The paper pointed out that the initial decision to carry out this research was prompted and partly funded by the Swedish parliament (50%) and partly by the Swedish sugar, chocolate and sweet manufacturers (50%). Further government funding was denied on ethical grounds by parliament following publication of the first report in 1953. The paper acknowledges that such a study would not be allowed to take place today.

Mass medication – the fluoride debate

The code of ethical conduct outlined by the General Dental Council (see Chapter 5) is based on a practical, normative approach to the regulation of right and wrong conduct by dental professionals. The following principles identify our responsibility to develop the good habits that dental professionals should acquire, the duties that we should follow, and the consequences of our behaviour on others:

- Put patients' interests first and act to protect them.

- Respect patient dignity and choice.

- Co-operate with other members of the dental team and other healthcare colleagues in the interest of the patient.

- Maintain professional knowledge and competence.

- Be trustworthy.

The first two principles provide some direction where there may be a need for the dental professional to become involved in examining specific controversial issues. An obvious example of this situation is that of supporting the adjustment of the levels of naturally occurring fluoride in the public water supply to an optimum level for the reduction of dental decay for the population in a designated area.

The desire to drink fluoride-free water is a personal preference and not a civil or human right and cannot be compared with issues such as free speech. In the UK we live in a society that expects us to consider communities as a whole, and this means that although we must consider personal and individual preferences as well as the best interests of others, as a society we are already used to accepting limits on free choice for the general good of others, for example, the wearing of seat-belts. If the four basic principles of ethics as identified by Beauchamp and Childress – autonomy, beneficence, non-maleficence and justice – are applied to the discussions around water fluoridation, there should be no difficulty for the dental team in justifying their contribution to the debate.

In addition, in a legal test case concerning water fluoridation in the High Court in Dublin, Ireland in 1986, Mr Justice Kenny stated that 'none of the personal rights of the citizen are unlimited – their exercise may be limited by Parliament when the common good requires this'. The following principles are the ones most commonly appealed to in applied ethical discussions:

- Personal benefit – Acknowledge the extent to which an action produces beneficial consequences for the individual in question.

- Social benefit – Acknowledge the extent to which an action produces beneficial consequences for society.

- Principle of benevolence – Help those in need.

- Principle of paternalism – Assist others in pursuing their best interests when they cannot do so themselves.

- Principle of harm – Do not harm others.

- Principle of honesty – Do not deceive others.

- Principle of lawfulness – Do not violate the law.

- Principle of autonomy – Acknowledge a person's freedom over his or her actions or physical body.

- Principle of justice – Acknowledge a person's right to due process, fair compensation for harm done, and fair distribution of benefits.

- Rights – Acknowledge a person's rights to life, information, privacy, free expression, and safety.

Conclusion

This book has been designed to help you ask questions, rather than to provide answers that will be appropriate in every ethical, legal or professional situation. As stated in earlier chapters, the GDC expects dental professionals to be ethical in their practice, up to date in their knowledge and skills, and aware of changes in legislation and guidelines. In the last chapter, we provide some suggestions for resources that might help you to stay well informed and up to date as far as ethics, law and professionalism are concerned. Any recommendations and additions will be gratefully received, and both included and acknowledged in future editions of this book.

We hope that you have found this book useful in helping to promote the ethical, legal and professional practice of dentistry and oral healthcare. Any omissions are of course ours, and we will seek to remedy them in future editions. Suggestions for improvements will be warmly welcomed, as will ethical, legal or professional case studies and scenarios to supplement those which we have provided in this edition of the book.

CHAPTER 10
RESOURCES AND SUGGESTED READING

CHAPTER 10
RESOURCES AND SUGGESTED READING

This chapter is intended to help you find resources which assist the teaching and learning of ethics, law and professionalism for dental professionals. We believe that this list is comprehensive and representative, but do not claim it is complete because new resources are created all the time; it should give an indication of the wide range of material that is available.

Dental organisations

General Dental Council
37 Wimpole Street
London W1G 8DQ
Tel: +44 (0) 20 7887 3800
Fax: +44 (0) 20 7224 3294

Email:
For general enquiries: Information@gdc-uk.org
For dental education enquiries: GDCeducation@gdc-uk.org
For dental care professional (DCP) education enquiries: DCP@gdc-uk.org
To report unregistered practitioners: IllegalPractice@gdc-uk.org

General Dental Council (GDC) resources:
All of the GDC documents which we have referred to in this book, as well as additional advice and updates, are available online at the GDC website (www.gdc-uk.org). These include:

General ethical guidance for current registrants –
        www.gdc-uk.org

Dealing with complaints from patients –
        www.dentalcomplaints.org.uk

The following GDC documents can all be accessed via this URL –
www.gdc-uk.org/News+publications+and+events/Publications.htm

- *The First Five Years – A Framework for Undergraduate Dental Education*
- *Developing the Dental Team*
- *Standards for Dental Professionals*
- *Principles of Dental Team Working*
- *Principles of Patient Consent*
- *Principles of Patient Confidentiality*
- *Principles of Complaints Handling*
- *Principles of Raising Concerns*

Dental professionals – membership organisations

British Dental Association
64 Wimpole Street
London W1G 8YS
Tel: +44 (0) 207 935 0875
Fax: +44 (0) 207 487 5232
Email: enquiries@bda.org
Advice and resources available at: www.bda-dentistry.org.uk/advice/index.cfm

British Dental Hygienists' Association
Mobbs Miller House
Ardington Road
Northampton NN1 5LP
Tel: +44 (0) 870 2430752
Email: enquiries@bdha.org.uk

British Association of Dental Therapists
Website: www.badt.org.uk

British Association of Dental Nurses
PO Box 4, Room 200
Hillhouse International Business Centre
Thornton-Cleveleys
FY5 4QD
Tel: +44 (0) 1253 338360
Website: www.badn.org.uk
Email: admin@badn.org.uk (for general enquiries)

Dental Technicians Association
PO Box 6520
Northampton
NN3 9ZX
Tel: +44 (0) 870 243 0753
Website: http://www.dta-uk.org
Email: sueadams@dta-uk.org

Orthodontic Technicians Association – UK
c/o Kerry Lancaster
Deputy Chief Instructor
Orthodontic Department
Eastman Dental Institute
256 Grays Inn Road
London
WC1X 8LD
Website: http://www.orthota.co.uk

British Dental Practice Managers Association
Osprey House
Primett Road
Stevenage
Hertfordshire
SG1 3EE
Tel: +44 (0) 870 840 0381
Fax: +44 (0) 870 840 0382
Email: info@bdpma.org.uk
Website: www.bdpma.org.uk

Dental protection organisations in the UK

Dental Defence Union
230 Blackfriars Road
London
SE1 8PJ
Tel: +44 (0) 20 7202 1500
Website: www.the-ddu.com
Email: ddu@the-ddu.com

Dental Protection Ltd
33 Cavendish Square
London
W1G 0PS
Tel: +44 (0) 20 7399 1400
Fax: +44 (0) 20 7399 1401
Website: www.dentalprotection.org
Email: enquiries@dentalprotection.org

Medical and Dental Defence Union of Scotland
Mackintosh House
120 Blythswood Street
Glasgow
G2 4EA
Tel: +44 (0) 141 221 5858
Fax: +44 (0) 141 228 1208
Website: www.mddus.com
Email: info@mddus.com

Suggested reading and resources

Chapter 5 (Use of clinical images)

British Medical Association – Taking and using visual and audio images of patients (www.bma.org.uk/ap.nsf/AttachmentsByTitle/PDFAVrecordings/$FILE/AV.pdf)

BMJ – Patient Consent Form for publication (http://bmj.bmjjournals.com/collections/informed_consent/draft_f.shtml)

BMJ – Revised Consent to Publication Guidelines (http://bmj.bmjjournals.com/advice/revised_guidelines2003.shtml)

General Medical Council – Making and Using Visual and Audio Recordings of Patients (www.gmc-uk.org/guidance/library/making_audiovisual.asp), May 2002.

Institute of Medical Illustrators (www.imi.org.uk/lawethics.htm). The Law and ethics page has useful links on consent, confidentiality, copyright, data protection, freedom of information, mobile phones, publishing and legislation.

Medical Defence Union – Warning on Use of Mobile Phones and Picture Messaging (www.the-mdu.com)

For further information on the ethical use of clinical images in healthcare practice, please contact Prof. John W B Bradfield*[†], Dr Adrian Longstaffe*, or Dr Jane Williams[†]

*Interactive Consultancies, 24 Clifton Wood Road, Clifton, Bristol, BS8 4TW

[†]E-learning Unit, Centre for Medical Education, University of Bristol, St Michael's Hill, Bristol BS2 8DZ

Chapter 7

Gould FK, Elliot TSJ, Foweraker J , Fulford M, Perry JD, Roberts GJ, Sandoe JAT, Watkin RW. 2006 (in press). Guidelines for the prevention of endocarditis: report of the Working Party of the British Society for Antimicrobial Chemotherapy, Journal for Antimicrobial Chemotherapy

Chapter 9 (research, audit and evidence-based practice)

- NHS Centre for Reviews and Dissemination (CRD) University of York, York, YO1 5DD

- *The Cochrane Library*, Update Software Ltd. Summertown Pavilion, Middle Way, Oxford, OX2 7LG www.cochrane.co.uk

- Scottish Intercollegiate Guidelines Network (www.sign.ac.uk/guidelines/)

- International Dental Federation (www.fdiworlddental.org/resources)

- *Evidence based Health Care:* how to make Health Policy and Management Decisions. JA Muir Gray. Edinburgh: Churchill Livingstone, 2001

- Bandolier, Hayward Medical Communications Bibliography – relevant to dental ethics, law and professionalism.

- Dent J, Harden R (eds). *A Practical Handbook for Medical Teachers*, 2nd edition. Edinburgh: Churchill Livingstone, 2005.

General

Downie RS, Macnaughton J. *Clinical Judgement: Evidence in Practice*. Oxford: Oxford University Press, 2000.

European Scientific Cooperation Network 'Medicine and Human Rights' of the European Federation of Scientific Networks. The human rights, ethical and moral dimensions of health care. Council of Europe Publishing, 1998.

Kay EJ, Shearer AC, Bridgman AM, Humpris GM. *Integrated Dental Treatment Planning: A Case-based Approach*. Oxford: Oxford University Press, 2005.

Illingworth S. *Approaches to ethics in higher education: Teaching ethics across the curriculum*. Philosophical and Religious Studies Subject Centre (PRS-LSTN), 2004.

Dental ethics and law

D'Cruz. *Legal Aspects of Dental Practice*. Edinburgh: Churchill Livingstone, 2006.

Lambden P (ed). *Dental Law and Ethics*. Oxford: Radcliffe Medical Press, 2002.

Medical ethics and law

Baxter C-M, Brennan MG, Coldicott Y, Möller M. *The Practical Guide to Medical Ethics and Law*, 2nd edition. Knutsford: PasTest, 2005.

Campbell A, Gillett G, Jones G. *Medical Ethics*, 4th edition. Oxford: Oxford University Press, 2005.

De Cruz P. *Medical Law*. London: Sweet and Maxwell, 2005.

Kennedy IM, Grubb A. *Medical Law*, 3rd edition. London: Butterworths, 2000.

Mason JK, Laurie GT. *Mason and McCall Smith's Law and Medical Ethics*, 7th edition. Oxford: Oxford University Press, 2006.

Professionalism

Coles C, Fish D. *Medical Education: Developing a Curriculum for Practice*. Milton Keynes: Open University Press, 2006.

Eraut M. *Developing Professional Knowledge and Competence*. London: Falmer Press, 1994.

Fish D, Coles C. *Developing Professional Judgement in Health Care*. London: Butterworth Heineman, 1998.

Nicholls G. *Professional Development in Higher Education*. London: Kogan Page, 2001.

Picker Institute. http://www.pickereurope.org

Wear D, Bickel J (eds). *Educating for Professionalism*. Iowa: University of Iowa Press, 2000.

Law

Elliot C, Quinn F. *Criminal Law*, 3rd edition. London: Longman, 2000.

Other resources

Numerous other resources are available for the learning and teaching of dental ethics, law and professionalism. We suggest the following ideas:

- The media – TV, radio and the printed press all provide a rich resource of materials which can be used in teaching and learning.

- The Internet – judicious use of dentally related websites can often provide an even more up-to-date resource than books or journals.

- Your own cases and experiences.

- Students' cases and experiences.

- Patients' stories and experiences (known in the jargon of ethics as 'the patient narrative') – developing the use of expert patients and patient teachers might well pay dividends in your practice, clinic or school.

The authors would welcome further resource suggestions for future editions of this book.

APPENDICES

APPENDIX 1

Foreword

1 Now the Fitness to Practice Panel

2 The First Five Years. Publication of the GDC. Wimpole St. London. 2nd Edition.

3 Developing the Dental Team. Publication of the GDC. Wimpole St. London. 1st Edition.

4 ADEE & DentEd website: http://adee.dental.tcd.ie

APPENDIX 2

REFERENCES

Chapter 3

1 Hilton SR, Slotnick HB. Proto-professionalism: how professionalisation occurs across the continuum of medical education. *Medical Education* 2005; **39**: 58–65.

2 Bertolami CN. Why our ethics curricula don't work. *Journal of Dental Education* 2004; **68**: 414–425.

3 Eggly S, Brennan S, Wiese-Rometsch W. 'Once when I was on call ...' Theory versus reality in training for professionalism. *Academic Medicine* 2005; **80**: 371–375.

4 Rose GL, Rukstalis MR, Schuckit MA. Informal mentoring between faculty and medical students. *Academic Medicine* 2005; **80**: 344–348.

5 Steinert Y, Cruess S, Cruess R, Snell L. Faculty development for teaching and evaluating professionalism: from programme design to curriculum change. *Medical Education* 2005; **39**: 127–136.

6 Huddle TS. Viewpoint: teaching professionalism: is medical morality a competency? *Academic Medicine* 2005; **80**: 885–891.

7 Chambers DW. The role of dentists in dentistry. *Journal of Dental Education* 2001; **65**: 1430–1440.

8 Rees C. Proto-professionalism and the three questions about development. *Medical Education* 2005; **39**: 9–11.

9 General Dental Council. *The First Five Years*. London: General Dental Council, 2002.

10 Standards Guidance. London: General Dental Council, 2005.

11 General Dental Council. *Developing the Dental Team. Curricula Frameworks for Registrable Qualifications for Professionals Complementary to Dentistry (PCDs)*. London: General Dental Council, 2004.

12 General Dental Council Press Release 19 September 2005 (see www.gdc-uk.org).

13 Hannah A, Millichamp CJ, Ayers KMS. A communication skills course for undergraduate dental students. *Journal of Dental Education* 2004; **68**: 970–977.

14 Rubin RW. Developing cultural competence and social responsibility in preclinical dental students. *Journal of Dental Education* 2004: **68**; 460–467.

15 Norwell N. The ten commandments of record keeping. *Journal of the Medical Defence Union* 1997; **13**: 8–9.

16 Medical Protection Society. *Keeping Medical Records. A Complete Guide for Students*. Medical Protection Society, 2002. www.mps.org.uk

17 Zarkowski P, Graham B. A four-year curriculum in professional ethics and law for dental students. *Journal of the American College of Dentists* 2001; **68**: 22–26.

Chapter 4

1   Veloski JJ, Fields SK, Boex JR, Blank LL. Measuring professionalism: a review of studies with instruments reported in the literature between 1982 and 2002. *Academic Medicine* 2005; **80**: 366–370.

2   Standards Guidance. London: General Dental Council, 2005.

3   Shrank WH, Reed VA, Jernstedt C. Fostering professionalism in medical education. A call for improved assessment and meaningful incentives. *Journal of General Internal Medicine* 2004; **19**: 881–892.

4   Bryan RE, Krych AJ, Carmichael SW, Viggiano TR, Pawlina W. Assessing professionalism in early medical education: experience with peer evaluation and self-evaluation in the gross anatomy course. *Annals of the Academy of Medicine Singapore* 2005; **34**: 486–491.

5   Shue CK, Arnold L, Stern DT. Maximising participation in peer assessment of professionalism: the students speak. *Academic Medicine* 2005; **80** (10 Supplement): S1–S5.

6   Musick DW, McDowell SM, Clark N, Salcido R. Pilot study of 360-degree assessment instrument for physical medicine and rehabilitation residency programs. *American Journal of Physical Medicine and Rehabilitation* 2003; **82**: 394–402.

7   Hurst YK, Prescott-Clements LE, Rennie JE. The patient assessment questionnaire: a new instrument for evaluating the interpersonal skills of vocational dental practitioners. *British Dental Journal* 2004; **197**: 497–500.

8   DeHaes JC, Oort FJ, Hulsman RL. Summative assessment of medical students' communication skills and professional attitudes through observation in clinical practice. *Medical Teacher* 2005; **27**: 583–589.

Chapter 8

1   Irvine D. Professionalism in the aftermath of the Shipman enquiry. Presented at a workshop of the Association for the Study of Medical Education on Defining Developing Professionalism. April 2005, London.

2   Schwartz B. Dental ethics: our future lies in education and ethics committees. *Journal of the Canadian Dental Association* 2004; **70**: 85–86.

3   Institute for International Medical Education. 'Professionalism' www.iime.org/glossary.htm (accessed June 2005).

4   Welie JVM. Is dentistry a profession? Part 2. The hallmarks of professionalism. *Journal of the Canadian Dental Association* 2004; **70**: 599–602.

5   Welie JVM. Is dentistry a profession? Part 3. Future challenges. *Journal of the Canadian Dental Association* 2004; **70**: 675–678.

6   Institute of Business Ethics. www.ibe.org.uk (accessed July 2005).

7   *A First Class Service: Quality in the New NHS.* Welsh Office, 1998.

Chapter 9

1   National Institute for Health and Clinical Excellence. http://www.nice.org.uk/ (accessed March 2006).

2   Smith R (ed) *Audit in Action.* London: BMJ Publishers, 1992.

3   Oliver RG. Audit – Whither or wither? [Guest Editorial]. *British Journal of Orthodontics* 1997; **24**: 247.

4   Economic and Social Research Council. Research Ethics Framework. www.esrcsocietytoday.ac.uk (accessed March 2006).

5   Hardman E, Joughin C. *Focus on Clinical Audit in Child and Adolescent Mental Health Services*, Ch 1: Clinical Audit: What it is and what it isn't. London: Royal College of Psychiatrists, 1998

6   http://www.wma.net/e/policy/b3.htm

7   MRS Professional Standards. www.mrs.org.uk/standards/children.htm (accessed March 2006).

8   The British Sociological Association website (www.britsoc.co.uk).

9   Medical Research Council. *MRC Ethics Guide. Medical research involving children.*
    London: MRC, 2004. www.mrc.ac.uk/pdf-ethics_guide_children.pdf (accessed
    March 2006).

10 Ess C and the AoIR Ethics Working Committee. Ethical decision-making and
    Internet research: Recommendations from the aoir ethics working committee,
    2002 (www.aoir.org/reports/ethics.pdf).

11 Related link The Hinxton Group. An International Consortium on Stem Cells,
    Ethics and Law.
    www.bep.ox.ac.uk/word%20files/the%20Hinxton%20Group%20Statement.doc /
    (accessed March 2006).

12 Marris E. Should journals police scientific fraud? *Nature* 2006; **439**: 520–521.

13 Martinson BC, Anderson MA, de Vries R. Scientists behaving badly. *Nature* 2005;
    435: 737–738.

14 Sackett D. Evidence-based medicine: What it is and what it isn't. Editorial *BMJ*
    1996, 312; 71–72

15 Gustaffson BE, Quensel CE, Lanke LS, Lundquist C, Grahnen H, Bonow BE, Krasse
    B. The Vipeholm dental caries study. The effect of different levels of
    carbohydrate intake on caries activity in 436 individuals observed for five years.
    Acta Odontologica Scandinavica 1954; **11**: 232–364.

16 Krasse B. The Vipeholm Dental Caries Study: recollections and reflections
    50 years later. *Journal of Dental Research* 2001; **80**: 1785–1788.

Chapter 9 – Further reading

- Davies PT, Dawes M, Seers K, Snowball R. *Evidence-Based Practice. A Primer for
  Health Care Professionals.* London: Churchill Livingstone, 1999, pp. 1–7.

- McKibbon K, Walter-Dilks C. Beyond ACP Journal Club: how to harness
  MEDLINE to solve clinical problems. *American College of Physicians Journal
  Club* 1994; **120** (suppl 2): A10–A12.

- Moles D, Silva IS. Causes, Associations and evaluating evidence; can we trust
  what we read? *Evidence Based Dentistry* 2000; **2**: 75–78.

INDEX